# This book is for you if you are seeking to:

- Know what Judaism offers beyond rules of "Thou shall ..." and "Thou shall not...."

- Discover Jewish teachings that will make a difference in your life.

- Explore a Jewish framework for reaching truthful decisions and taking meaningful actions.

- Learn how the rabbis have interpreted the Hebrew Bible through the centuries.

- Find a positive model for respectful disagreement when opinions differ.

- Appreciate a Jewish perspective on what may be called "conscience," "moral agency," "personal autonomy," or "informed will."

- Understand why the Hebrew Bible that wants us to tell the truth illustrates its teachings with stories of people who lie.

- Identify what Jews across denominations and communities have in common.

- Build a meaningful personal Jewish life.

- Draw from Jewish teachings to grow your own beliefs, whatever your background or spiritual commitment.

Other Books by Rabbi Dennis S. Ross

*God in Our Relationships: Spirituality between People from the
    Teachings of Martin Buber*
*All Politics Is Religious: Speaking Faith to the Media, Policy Makers
    and Community*

when a
# LIE
## is NOT a
# SIN

The Hebrew Bible's
Framework
for Deciding

## RABBI DENNIS S. ROSS

*For People of All Faiths, All Backgrounds*

**JEWISH LIGHTS Publishing**

Woodstock, Vermont

*When a Lie Is Not a Sin:*
*The Hebrew Bible's Framework for Deciding*

2016 Quality Paperback Edition, First Printing
© 2016 by Dennis S. Ross

**Library of Congress Cataloging-in-Publication Data**
Names: Ross, Dennis S. (Dennis Sidney), 1953– author.
Title: When a lie is not a sin : the Hebrew Bible's framework for deciding /
    Rabbi Dennis S. Ross.
Description: Woodstock, VT : Jewish Lights Publishing, [2016] | ©2016 | Includes
    bibliographical references.
Identifiers: LCCN 2016007170| ISBN 9781580238588 (pbk.) |
    ISBN 9781580238656 (ebook)
Subjects: LCSH: Truthfulness and falsehood—Biblical teaching. | Sin—Biblical
    teaching. | Bible. Old Testament—Criticism, interpretation, etc.
Classification: LCC BS1199.T7 R67 2016 | DDC 296.3/673—dc23
LC record available at http://lccn.loc.gov/2016007170

10 9 8 7 6 5 4 3 2 1

Manufactured in the United States of America
Cover Design: Jenny Buono
Cover Art: © Gigra from Shutterstock.com
Interior Design: Tim Holtz

*For People of All Faiths, All Backgrounds*
Published by Jewish Lights Publishing
A Division of LongHill Partners, Inc.
Sunset Farm Offices, Route 4, P.O. Box 237
Woodstock, VT 05091
Tel: (802) 457-4000   Fax: (802) 457-4004
www.jewishlights.com

*To Joshua, Adam, and Miriam,*
*Your lives bless ours.*

# Contents

# The Examined Jewish Life

When it comes to the Hebrew Bible, a lie is not necessarily a sin.

Drought and famine strike the land of Canaan, forcing Abraham and Sarah to flee to Egypt to get food and avoid starvation. Fearing that the border authorities will kill a husband and abduct a wife into the harem, Abraham asks Sarah to join him in saying that they are siblings instead of spouses. Bad news for Sarah—she will wind up in the harem either way—but that scheme saves Abraham's life.

I was a six-year-old yeshiva student when I first read this story. The class learned to translate the original Hebrew into Yiddish phrase by phrase, leaving me to turn it all into English on my own in my head. But that story of Sarah and Abraham didn't sit well with me in any language, even back then. I couldn't understand why God allowed the Promised Land to descend into famine and Sarah land in a harem, all that without even a word of protest from Abraham. What's more, Abraham and Sarah lied about their relationship, and telling a lie was the last thing I ever expected anyone in the Hebrew Bible to do.

Our rabbis also struggle with the story and these questions. Some rabbis justify the lie by claiming it saved Abraham's life;

others say it isn't a lie at all. Elsewhere, as I later learned, the Hebrew Bible says that Sarah and Abraham really are brother and sister, children of the same father but different mothers (Genesis 20:12). But even with these explanations, what about the Hebrew Bible's other lies? Jacob deceives his father, Joseph hides his identity from his brothers, and more.

The Hebrew Bible's detractors certainly know what to say. Anti-Semites seize on this story, and stories like it, as an excuse to smear all Jews as selfish and untrustworthy. Others use these stories of lies to dismiss the Hebrew Bible and Judaism entirely. And these lies continued to bother me as I read and studied this Torah portion, Shabbat after Shabbat, year after year, until I eventually realized that though Abraham and Sarah lied, their lie was not a sin. Famine struck Canaan, life in the Promised Land fell short of its promise, and lying became the most truthful thing any person in that impossible situation could do.

It sounds hypocritical for the Hebrew Bible to demand truth on one hand and chronicle untruthful behavior on the other. A casual reader might come away confused by the Hebrew Bible's lesson to "do as I command," that is, uphold the truth, and "don't do as they do," that is, avoid the falsehood described therein. The reality is that the Hebrew Bible's mixed message about truth and falsehood provides a framework for deciding whether or not a lie is a sin.

## How This Book Came to Be

I didn't realize that I was on my way to writing a book many years ago when I sat down to read *Lying: Moral Choice in Public and Private Life* by Harvard University philosophy professor Sissela Bok.[1] I was taken by how carefully and thoughtfully Professor Bok organized and considered different kinds of lies—lies told to protect ourselves and others, lies told to children and the sick, lies intended to safeguard the public interest, and more. Until then, I assumed that it was always wrong to lie—although there wasn't much harm in stretching the truth to spare someone's feelings or to avoid an embarrassing situation. Professor Bok helped me to gain a deeper understanding of truth, the different kinds of lies, and the nuances and significance of each one. She also helped me understand why the Hebrew Bible wants us to tell the truth on the one hand, yet includes stories of lies on the other.

My experience as a pastoral counselor and my training as a social worker also contributed to the ideas about making decisions that I delve into in this book. A person seeks a clergyperson's counsel for support, whether facing a challenging decision, curious about spiritual direction, or for a host of other reasons. As a pastoral counselor, I listen, consider Jewish perspectives, and may reflect on the issues presented or recommend a course of action, but I never decide for someone else, out of the humility and recognition that a counselee, not the pastoral counselor, is the one who has to live with the consequences of acting on a decision. I also draw from my experience as an instructor of medical ethics and a religious advocate for reproductive health care. All this brings me back to the Hebrew Bible's respect for our wisdom to reach and act upon personal decisions about Jewish belief, practice, and living.

This book also grows out of my previous books, *God in Our Relationships: Spirituality between People from the Teachings of Martin Buber* (Jewish Lights Publishing),[2] which identifies spiritual opportunities in the daily routine, as well as *All Politics Is Religious: Speaking Faith to the Media, Policy Makers and Community* (SkyLight Paths Publishing),[3] a handbook for defining and communicating spiritual and social values.

All told, the difference between truth and falsehood is often clear and simple. But when life gets complicated, the Hebrew Bible is a guide for those times, too, as a partner for those of us living the examined Jewish life.

# Introduction

# Hiding in Plain Sight

The Hebrew Bible so loves the truth that if it were a letter from a friend, it would be signed, "Yours truly," because the Hebrew Bible tells the truth even when its favorite people lie. Please don't get the wrong impression about the founders of Judaism. They were honest and upright, for the most part. But pioneers of other religions lived perfect lives. What happened to ours?

To be sure, the Hebrew Bible is true and it demands the truth, but in a puzzling turn, the Hebrew Bible actually rewards some lies and lets others go unpunished. For instance, when Abraham and Sarah decide to lie about their marriage with "We're sibs," the Hebrew Bible not only smiles on that lie, it goes on to brag that the early Hebrews are eventually blessed to walk away from that incident with a caravan full of swag. The way the Hebrew Bible speaks about that story, it's as if telling that lie was the best thing that anyone in the Hebrew Bible ever did.

For those of us who equate religion and truthfulness, it's unsettling to read how nimbly our spiritual ancestors would spin a yarn and how often the Hebrew Bible leaves us to think that they get away with it. There's no attempt to cover up or whitewash when Jacob dresses up as his brother to fool their father. You have to read ahead and pay close attention to see that the Hebrew

Bible disapproves. I wanted the Hebrew Bible to explicitly distance itself on the spot or at least offer a disclaimer, like this: "For educational purposes only. Don't you dare try this under your roof!" What's more, the book I imagine signed, "Yours truly," the Hebrew Bible that urges us to "keep far from falsehood" (Exodus 23:7), unashamedly, even proudly, describes all kinds of lies—little and big; deception, denial, and less than full disclosure; lies to children, spouses, and a head of state. There's bald-faced lying to God, even as God goes out of the way to be totally honest. And, as we shall see, God shades the truth, too. To top that off, our rabbis establish a weekly Torah schedule that has us read and reread these stories, year after year, as if wanting to make sure we know that the people in the Hebrew Bible lie. Let's give the Hebrew Bible credit for honesty, but all that candor about a lack of candor leaves us questioning why a truthful Hebrew Bible would showcase less than truthful behavior. But before I get too far ahead of myself, let's go back and acknowledge that the Hebrew Bible explicitly highlights those stories for all to see; we just breeze by the lying and let it hide in very plain sight.

We let the lies go hiding when a court witness places a hand on a Bible and promises "to tell the truth, the whole truth, and nothing but the truth, so help me God" and no one even blinks. The lies hide again when elected officials take office and pretty much do the same. You have to wonder if the faithful among them ever opened the book they're swearing on, let alone looked inside. To be sure, the Hebrew Bible sometimes gets harsh and strident when biblical figures break the rules. But other times, the text appears to give us implicit permission to ignore the violations.

The Hebrew Bible makes it very easy to overlook the lies, with that deadpan delivery that takes simple language to describe what happens and leaves it to the reader to decide whether or not someone has misbehaved. What's more, the Hebrew Bible is a great entertainer, cleverly engaging an audience by grabbing our attention with amusing tidbits of "behind-the-scenes" reporting of our spiritual ancestors' doings, all this distracting attention from the mixed message of falsehood embedded in the truth. I imagine a merchant on camelback showing up at an oasis with a load of goods from a foreign land and a traveling salesman's collection of stories, as our tent-dwelling spiritual ancestors bend over in knee-slapping laughter to evening campfire tales about a scheme between midwives that fools the powerful leadership of Egypt or about a younger brother dressing up as the elder to bamboozle a blessing out of a father. I don't think it's at all disrespectful to say that ancient Torah study was the late-night entertainment of its day, with a biblical text instead of a host's monologue that warms the audience to a religious message in lieu of a punch line. Just as we do, our ancestors happily fell for the Hebrew Bible's suspense-creating literary strategy, designed to lead a reader to wonder, "He did what? Will he get away with it? What if the lie is discovered?" No wonder the Hebrew Bible is a popular and enduring book! The Hebrew Bible, then, is honest about the dishonesty, especially when it comes to the lies and we fall for that "Watch my other hand" strategy of distraction and turn to other issues in the text.

There's another reason to shy away from talking about the lying: our founders' behavior shines an uncomfortable light on our own. Who wants to do all the heavy lifting of judging ourselves in the light of the complicated legacy of our religious forebears? It's easier to turn the page or roll the scroll than to take the Hebrew Bible as a moral mirror and microscope to highlight and examine the times when we fall short. But before we get too hard on the people in the Hebrew Bible or on ourselves, let's return to the point of this book: each lie occurs under complicated moral circumstances in which, yes, it may even be a religious imperative to lie.

Truth telling is often simple and straightforward, no complications involved. But when life demands more than just, "This is right, that's wrong, case closed," the Hebrew Bible is a guide for those times, too. This book presents the Hebrew Bible's framework for approaching some of the most difficult life circumstances. It raises thoughtful questions and offers practical suggestions about truth and falsehood in a way that will make a difference in how we live our lives.

## The Hebrew Bible as a Framework

To speak of the Hebrew Bible as a "framework" is to take the book as our loving companion along the path to building a Jewish life. The Hebrew Bible doesn't dictate or decide for us; it supports each of us as we gather facts, think things through, and reach and act on conclusions that lead to Jewish living. That's different than saying the Hebrew Bible is a "rule book" that expects a person to behave in one particular way and no other. If you're up to considering the Hebrew Bible as a framework, you'll also appreciate that it offers differing perspectives when it comes to God.

Just mentioning the God of the Hebrew Bible brings up that old man in the sky, spewing fire and brimstone, the kind of judgmental and punishing heavenly personality some religious people spend so much time talking about these days. To be sure, we'll find this portrait of God in the Hebrew Bible. We'll also find other ideas to consider, just as I noted in my earlier book, *God in Our Relationships: Spirituality between People from the Teachings of Martin Buber* (Jewish Lights Publishing), which sees God's grace in everyday human experience. Taking the Hebrew Bible as a framework is less about being judgmental and more about the importance of spirituality in our relationships and decision making. There is much more to say about God. Stay tuned.

## Perspectives about Decision Making

A Jewish framework is about decision making. It relies on the religious importance of what is called "moral agency," "conscience," "personal autonomy," and "free will" and being open-minded about people and their differing conclusions. This open-minded perspective conflicts with the popular assumption that a religious person is, by definition, a very judgmental person. On one hand, dismissing all religious people as judgmental is, in and of itself, a judgment that does not always bear itself out in fact. The reality is that all of us judge others, whether we're religious or not. Moreover, I'm more interested in how we handle the judgments we make and less concerned whether or not we judge.

My last book, *All Politics Is Religious: Speaking Faith to the Media, Policy Makers and Community* (SkyLight Paths Publishing), drew a line when it comes to imposing unwanted religious judgments onto the private lives of others who follow their own faith teachings or conscience. So, there will be times that I judge and times that I know that your conscience must rule when you make private, personal life decisions.

At the end of the day, it's important to recognize that there is more to God and religion than passing judgment on others. As strongly as I assert and defend my opinions, I also know that I am not the boss of your life. I can only decide for myself. After all, each of us is a descendent of Adam and Eve. We inherit the legacy of their decision to eat from the Tree of Knowledge in the Garden of Eden; we taste that fruit each time we open our eyes and make a decision. Our spiritual inheritance is also evident when we turn inward for self-examination on Shabbat and in the deeper reflection of the High Holy Days—these are just a couple of examples of how we take life seriously in the light of the Hebrew Bible and go on to chart a thoughtful and Jewish life direction. The responsibility to arrive at personal decisions rests on each one of us.

## Perspectives on Differences and Common Ground

Some critics will dismiss this emphasis on personal decision making as a "do your own thing," "anything goes," "easy way out," and "cherry picking" kind of religion. The reality is that in a free and diverse society like ours, each of us makes our own religious decisions, whether our religious leaders approve of them or not. A religious leader can encourage people and support them but must draw the line at bullying. No one has the religious responsibility or authority to order others around or to write their personal religious restrictions into the law of the land. So there will be diversity among all faiths as well as among Jewish denominations and, just as critically, within them— each one of them—especially in our varied and democratic nation.

The reality is that we don't all believe the same thing deep down inside. Different faiths really do have different teachings, and those differences matter. Being honest about spirituality and religion means respecting those differences and avoiding broad statements intended to sweep all those disagreements under the rug. Of course, people can come to their own truth through any number of paths, within Judaism and elsewhere. This book recognizes that Judaism offers a unique outlook, unlike any other. It begins by encouraging decision making within a Jewish framework in order to arrive at authentic Jewish living.

Finally, I firmly believe that religion is more about uniting and less about dividing. There are many good reasons for the popular saying "Never discuss religion in polite company." Religious differences do breed arguments. But you don't have to look far to tamp down the squabbling. The bickering suddenly and remarkably ends when we come to the lying in the Hebrew Bible; just about everyone agrees that a lie is a lie, whether told by the Hebrew midwives, Jacob, or anyone else. People will always differ over religion. They'll disagree as to whether or not the Hebrew Bible is true, and if they think it's true, they'll debate what that truth happens to be. But if you want to find common ground across the Jewish spectrum and among a variety of faiths, start with these lies, which is exactly what this book is about.

## How This Book Is Organized

This book has four parts. Part 1 opens with a discussion of truth: how much the Hebrew Bible loves the truth and wants us to tell it.

It also considers different kinds of truth—scientific, historical, and spiritual, and especially Jewish spiritual truth. Parts 2 and 3 consider falsehood through the eyes of the Hebrew Bible and its interpreters, especially the Midrash and rabbinic commentators, all in a modern light. Part 2 examines "little" lies, including lies intended to cover up small social miscues and contribute to peace in the home and among friends, as well as lies that embellish the truth, half-truths, and lies told out of benevolent paternalism. A brief chapter of analysis recognizes that while a lie is not necessarily a sin, every lie, large or small, has a consequence. Part 3 examines "bigger" lies, including lies told in self-protection, lies seeking self-advancement, lies told to punish, the duty to tell the truth, and lies that serve noble purposes. Part 4 covers the Hebrew Bible's framework for reaching truthful decisions. It draws from my experience as a rabbi, a pastoral counselor, a social worker, and an instructor of medical ethics to show the importance of personal decision making in health care, social living, and Jewish life.

We'll move from there to acknowledge the importance of free will and personal responsibility in the Jewish tradition, how one-of-a-kind Jewish perspectives open doors to the distinctive way of Jewish living that builds common religious ground. Above all, we will see that there are times when telling a lie is sometimes the most truthful thing a person can do and that the Hebrew Bible gives us a framework for figuring out when those times happen to be.

# Part I

# Truth

## Chapter 1

# The Hebrew Bible Is True

In a scene Moses never imagined, a California pastor's tweet, "Costco has Bibles for sale under the genre of FICTION," ignited a national Twitterstorm of controversy.[1] The embarrassed Costco retail management blamed a distributor for a labeling error and then said, "We take responsibility and should have caught the mistake. We are correcting this with them for future distribution. In addition, we are immediately relabeling all the mislabeled Bibles. We greatly apologize for this error." The words of remorse satisfied some but only stoked the rage of others who believed that a "fiction" label is precisely what the Bible deserves.

"I fail to see the problem," said one social media critic. "Costco got it right," by calling the Bible "fiction."

"Costco should have kept the label," someone else noted. "And stuck it next to a book about unicorns and leprechauns."

Another chimed in, "People who work in bookstores have to constantly deal with customers who think it's hilarious to move Bibles to the 'Fiction' section."

There were similar verbal squalls at our family gatherings whenever Uncle Lou, of blessed memory, unapologetically called the Bible "fiction," too. Uncle Lou swore that he had no need for God, the Hebrew Bible, or Jewish traditions. He never came to Passover seders or bar or bat mitzvahs. As for the Hebrew Bible?

"It's full of lies. I don't believe it." I can only imagine the thunder-bolt he would have thrown into the Costco social media tempest.

Like Lou, many people are convinced that the Bible is "fiction." As for moral truth, "You don't need the Bible to know that it's wrong to murder or steal," they say. "Figure it out on your own." The issue of biblical truthfulness enters many more corners of popular life. In contrast to Uncle Lou, George and Ira Gershwin artfully raised the issue in their musical classic *Porgy and Bess* with "The things that you're liable to read in the Bible, it ain't necessarily so." But I sure was surprised when this question wormed its way into the 2008 Republican presidential debate.

CNN's Anderson Cooper moderated a first, a presidential debate featuring ordinary Americans questioning candidates via YouTube.[2] We heard and saw one questioner introduce himself as follows:

> I'm Joseph. I'm from Dallas, Texas. And how you answer this question will tell us everything we need to know about you. Do you believe every word of this book? (He holds up a Bible.) And I mean specifically this book that I'm holding in my hand. Do you believe this book?

Here is some of what the candidates said:

> *Mayor Rudy Giuliani*: I believe it, but I don't believe it necessarily literally true in every single respect. I think there are parts of the Bible that are interpretive. It does define, to a very large extent, my faith.

> *Governor Mitt Romney*: I believe the Bible is the word of God, absolutely.... It's a guide for my life and for hundreds of millions, billions of people around the world.

> *Governor Mike Huckabee*: Sure, I believe the Bible is exactly what it is. It's the word of revelation to us from God

himself.... I think what the question tried to make us feel like was that, well, if you believe the part that says, "Go and pluck out your eye"—well, none of us believe that we ought to go pluck out our eye. That obviously is allegorical. But the Bible has some messages that nobody really can confuse and really not left up to interpretation: "Love your neighbor as yourself." ... Until we get those simple, real easy things right, I'm not sure we ought to spend a whole lot of time fighting over the other parts that are a little bit complicated.... There are parts of it I don't fully comprehend and understand, but I'm not supposed to, because the Bible is a revelation of an infinite God, and no finite person is ever going to fully understand it.

I sure appreciated the responses and consensus. The Bible is true—literally in some places, poetically in others. I also respected the way they said the Bible includes things we don't understand, at least not yet, bringing me to think of stories about talking animals, such as the serpent of Eden or Balaam's ass, the kind of stories that rankled Uncle Lou.

The reality is that no presidential candidate—Democrat or Republican, not even the pastor among them—could provide a full-hearted consideration of biblical truth in the assigned ninety seconds. But the bigger issue is, really, what difference does it make whether a president believes the Bible's "every word" or not? Article 6 of the United States Constitution says that "no religious test shall ever be required as a qualification to any office or public trust under the United States." That is to say, you don't need to be of a particular faith—or any faith—to hold office; there's no religious "litmus test." So, it's hard to figure out what Joseph from Dallas had in mind when he said, "How you answer this question will tell us everything we need to know." Given the wording of the Constitution, a candidate's religion doesn't tell us a thing—not at all—and it's hard to figure out why the debate's screeners allowed this question through. What's more, this was a presidential debate, not a church, synagogue, or mosque search committee interview. We were electing a president, not a pastor!

# Which Bible?

But I digress. Let's get back to the topic by saying that I believe that the Hebrew Bible is entirely true; there's truth in each and every word. But before we go any further, let's consider this: Which Bible are we discussing? Governor Romney's Bible is not Mayor Giuliani's, nor is Governor Huckabee's Bible the same as mine. One Bible includes the New Testament and another doesn't. The Qur'an is holy to some, but not to others. So, when we talk about the Bible's truth, we have to ask, "Which Bible do you mean?"

This book is about the Hebrew Bible, particularly the first part of the Hebrew Bible, the Torah, the Five Books of Moses—Genesis, Exodus, Leviticus, Numbers, and Deuteronomy—that is to say, the first of the Hebrew Bible's three sections. The second section, the Prophets, includes books like Joshua, Kings, Samuel, Isaiah, and Jeremiah. The third section, the Writings, has Proverbs, Jonah, Esther, Job, and more. That's the Hebrew Bible. Now let's focus on the Torah.

The word "Torah" in the broadest sense means many different things beyond the Five Books of Moses. The Torah refers to the scroll in the ark, as well as the book we use in Torah study class, the sum total of Jewish thinking and writing, and the Jewish way of life. This book draws from all of those definitions of "Torah," whether bound in print, rolled on parchment, or lived in life. It takes the body of Jewish literature, Jewish history, and how Jews act today to create a framework for Jewish living.

The Hebrew Bible began as spoken Hebrew that was eventually written down in a scroll. Most people read the Hebrew Bible in translation, in their own language—English, or whatever that reader's language happens to be—and, as with any translation, something is guaranteed to get lost going from one language into the other. First of all, the Hebrew Bible's Hebrew is at times unclear, so even the best translation falls short. Beyond that, each translator brings a personal bias. Some of these biases don't amount to much; other disagreements will flare up when an entire religious outlook rests on just a few words.

For instance, many assume the Hebrew Bible insists that sex came on the scene only after Adam and Eve ate from the Tree of Knowledge of Good and Evil in the Garden of Eden. That's to say that there was no sex before the "fall." But some of the most respected rabbinic commentators, Rashi and others, read the Bible's Hebrew differently. They conclude that Adam and Eve conceived and gave birth to their first child, Cain, before eating the fruit. The first couple had sex, right there in Eden. We'll look at this issue more deeply, later on. For now, let's note that an important religious difference rests on this difference in translation and interpretation. Any conversation about the Hebrew Bible's truth must acknowledge that each translator has his or her own approach to the original text. This book contains my own Hebrew-to-English translations of the Hebrew Bible and the writings of the rabbis, and as you might expect, I have my point of view, too. Speaking of the rabbis, let's turn to them right now.

## The Hebrew Bible Includes the Voices of the Rabbis

When I talk about "the rabbis" I mean the interpreters of the Hebrew Bible from before the beginning of the Common Era, through the Middle Ages, to today. The rabbis compiled their teachings in books like the Mishnah, the Talmud, and the Midrash and many other volumes of laws and commentaries. The rabbis defined, nurtured, and strengthened Judaism through the centuries. They also gave us a remarkable model for respectful dialogue about religion, especially when we disagree. The rabbis set a high standard for talking about it.

The rabbis don't avoid controversy, even over the most delicate and sensitive of matters. They plunge right into it; they don't shy away. They freely disagree and take those disagreements as an opportunity to open purposeful and respectful conversation that honors the integrity of each other and the importance of the matters under consideration. They argue and reach conclusions, if not consensus. Critically, they record their many conversations—all sides and verbatim, including majority and minority opinions—out of respect for one another and for further learning through the generations. Their insights, combined with their model of learning and respectful dissent, set the table for our modern ways of Torah study, one of the most engaging, challenging, and gratifying Jewish opportunities today. All too often, people unfortunately equate "organized religion" with angry disagreement and little else. By contrast, the rabbis give us a model for candid conversation and cooperation across religious lines, a model we honor at each Torah study Shabbat morning, week after week.

Finally, the rabbis of the Talmud went out of their way to promote their teachings. Unlike some religious traditions that kept the truth secret among a privileged inner circle or restricted ritual practice to a small number of the faithful, the rabbis didn't keep their understanding of the Hebrew Bible to themselves. They democratized the faith by putting the Hebrew Bible and their teachings into the hands of the people, literally and figuratively. They popularized Jewish knowledge in order to empower individuals to take charge of living their own Jewish lives. They also gave us the framework we need for wise decision making today.

So the Hebrew Bible is true—there's truth in each and every word—as interpreted and taught by our rabbis. Now, we ask: What truth does the Hebrew Bible want us to know? For instance, does the Hebrew Bible want us to know that the world came to be in a certain way in a certain amount of time? Does it want us to know that our spiritual ancestors visited specific places and said specific things? Does it want us to believe that it rained on Noah and that

Moses split a sea by power of God's word and faith? Or does the Hebrew Bible have a different kind of truth in mind?

The next chapter looks at the Hebrew Bible's truth. It examines the differences between spiritual truth and other kinds of truth, as we prepare to enter the conversation about the significance of the times when people in the Hebrew Bible lie.

# Chapter 2

# The Hebrew Bible and the Truth

## Science, History, and Spirit

### Scientific Truth

I invited a dermatologist to lead Torah study when the weekly portion came to the skin diseases of Leviticus. I wanted an expert medical opinion on verses like these: "When a man or woman's skin is white and the priest sees the white discoloration appears to be dull white, a skin disease broke out. The person is clean" (Leviticus 13:38–39).

The doctor arrived with an armful of textbooks filled with photos of rashes, inflammations, and other afflictions of the skin and hair. One by one, he compared the Hebrew Bible's cases to those he studied and treats, and he concluded that the medical textbooks and the Hebrew Bible verses are not on the same page, leaving us to diagnose this dilemma: What should we do when science and religion are at odds? Fortunately, there's no need to choose one over the other.

Religion and health care were one and the same to the Hebrew Bible. Our portable desert sanctuary, the Tent of Meeting, was the health clinic of its day, the Israelites bringing their medical concerns to the priest. No one comes to temple to diagnose an odd-looking rash these days, yet faith still plays an important role in supporting and advancing healing and comfort. Good health was a religious matter in Hebrew Bible times, as it is now. Both science and religion play a role in wellness, and there is another Jewish spiritual truth in the health laws of the Hebrew Bible. In contrast to the very human inclination to permanently banish someone who looks different or isn't well, the laws of the Hebrew Bible instead outline rituals for restoring a healed person to the community (Leviticus 14). In its own time, the Hebrew Bible provided a path to reduce stigma and encourage inclusion. Today, however, balancing science and spirit remains a challenge. A recent Pew Forum survey found nearly six in ten people in the United States believe that religion and science often conflict, mostly over issues related to the origins of the universe and evolution.[1] While I'm with the four in ten who don't have a problem bridging physical and spiritual realities, I recognize that the natural order and the Hebrew Bible seem out of sync. Let's consider one example in the story of the ten plagues.

## The Ten Plagues and Science

The Egyptian Pharaoh refuses to free the enslaved people of Israel, so God inflicts plagues on Egypt ten times until Pharaoh relents. The plagues include water turning to blood, swarms of frogs covering the land, and more.

I don't pay much attention to scientific, philosophical, or theological concerns when dipping my finger into the wine and flicking ten drops—one for each plague—onto the edge of the dinner plate at the Passover seder. I'm having too much fun. It's only afterward and only occasionally that my ears perk up when someone says, "Moses really held out his walking staff and, before you knew it, the water turned to blood," while others argue, "It's all made up!"

Our rabbis also struggle with this religion-science-history conundrum. On one hand, they believe the universe is orderly and predictable, as reflected in the prayers handed down to us, for instance, praising God who each morning "makes light and creates darkness." At the same time, the rabbis believe that so-called "miracles" happen just as the Hebrew Bible describes, and they go out of their way to reconcile what appears to be a conflict.

Let's take one example of how the rabbis seek to strike that science-spirituality balance in the Mishnah (*Pirke Avot* 5:6). The rabbis ingeniously posit that God made all the miracles during the world's creation, at sunset, on the sixth day, just as Shabbat began. They then note that God placed the wonders on some kind of heavenly timer to launch precisely at the required moment, no suspension of nature's ways involved. The preprogrammed miracles include Balaam's talking ass, manna to feed the people of Israel in the Sinai wilderness, Noah's rainbow, and the miraculous walking staff Moses holds out over the Nile River to initiate the ten plagues. That's one religious explanation, a fancy way of saying, "Yes, we have no miracles." But this response doesn't put the question to bed, not at all. You're perfectly justified in wondering why Balaam's beast of burden speaks while all your dog does is growl and bark and, if you are a hiker tempted to compare yourself to Moses, wondering why lake water just sits there when you wave your walking stick above the surface.

This isn't just an academic question for the rabbis, any more than it is for us. The rabbis understand the realities of lived life. They know of our hopes, prayers, dreams, and soulful longing for miracles when facing significant personal challenges relating to family, work, faith, health, and more. They have the same yearnings in their own lives. Yet, all this storytelling from the rabbis might be enough to prompt you to start looking for a scientific explanation for miracles like the ten plagues, and we sure have those to turn to.

For instance, twentieth-century religious scholar Greta Hort proposes that the ten plagues came from a domino effect of natural causes, one bringing on the next.[2] The series of disasters began when unusually heavy mountain rainfalls washed large amounts of red, blood-colored mud into the Nile River and downstream, making water-based life unsustainable in the Nile Delta. Fish died in the muddied, swollen Nile, just as the Hebrew Bible describes. That was plague number one. The Nile's many frogs fled the dirty river water for dry land: plague two. The flooding disturbed and released dormant, poisonous anthrax spores that killed the frogs, whose decomposing bodies attracted insects: plagues three and four. Keep in mind all the distance between the tropical Nile Delta and the arid, desertlike Goshen region in Israel. Goshen is in a different place with a different climate, which explains why Israel was spared these plagues while Egypt suffered. Back to the anthrax, which caused the next, fifth plague of livestock disease, and the sixth plague of inflammation. Thus we have a scientific explanation for the first six plagues.

Next, in a coincidence, a catastrophic hailstorm, unrelated to the Nile water disaster sequence, made for plague seven. In another coincidence, a locust swarm left the land denuded and dry in plague eight, setting the stage for the horrible dust storm we know as plague number nine. As for Hort's overall thesis so far, we have a perfect storm of natural catastrophes, worthy of a Weather Channel special, if not a season series.

Come to the tenth plague, the death of the firstborn, Hort blames this on—oops!—a translation error. Hort says that that a correct translation would tell us that the "first fruits"—*bikkurim*—died, not the "firstborn sons"—*bechorim*. As a firstborn son myself, I can tell you, that's a relief. But in all seriousness, here's an example of how translation becomes an issue—first fruits versus firstborn—when taking the Hebrew Bible from one language to another.

So Hort sees a cascade of catastrophic environmental coincidences and consequences sending the Egyptian ecology out of whack. The people of the day spoke of "miracles" because, you could say, they had no other explanation. But before we take Hort's opinion as the final word of science, let's recognize that religious folks aren't the only ones to have their differences. There's disagreement among scientists, too.

Look at how N. Joel Ehrenkranz and Deborah Sampson argue that the first plague of "blood" had nothing to do with mud or anthrax.[3] An aberrant El Niño warming of the Mediterranean Sea sparked a red algae toxic bloom, resembling blood, and backflowed into the Nile Delta. That was plague one. The El Niño also triggered unusual rainfall that "initiated the serial catastrophes of biblical sequence,"[4] the next five plagues of frogs, lice, insects, cattle disease, and boils. Again, the environmental problems affected only coastal regions where the Egyptians lived, leaving Israel's interior region of Goshen untouched. Next, plagues six, seven, and eight, just as Hort suggests, rose from coincidental hailstorms and locust swarms. Plague nine wasn't a sandstorm, but fog resembling darkness. As for the tenth plague, the authors maintain that the firstborn sons of Egypt were served special foods that no one else got to eat. Unfortunately for Egypt's firstborn boys, the foods were badly contaminated and lethal: plague ten.

As you know by now, I'm not a scientist, but just as a scientist will have an opinion about religion, a religious person can weigh in on scientific explanations. That is to say, as a rabbi, I can tell you what I think when I read about scientific explanations for events in the Hebrew Bible: I don't get much soulful uplift wondering whether it was red mud or red algae. Putting these natural wonders under the clinical microscope might well explain something about the science—how an event happened, and when—but it doesn't cultivate that sense of wonder, awe, and enchantment and that aura of the mysterious that are so critical to a rich spiritual life.

So the scientists disagree, religious people disagree, and what's more, when it comes to the plagues, the Bible disagrees with itself, too. If you don't know already, the Bible contains three versions of the plagues. We've already discussed the first, and most popular, version, beginning in Exodus chapter 7. Two more versions appear in the Bible's book of Psalms, one in Psalm 78 and the other in

Psalm 105, and they disagree over the number of plagues, as well as their order and substance.

As we mentioned, the book of Exodus describes these ten plagues:

1. Blood
2. Frogs
3. Lice
4. Insects
5. Cattle disease
6. Boils afflicting people and animals
7. Hail
8. Locusts
9. Darkness
10. Death of the firstborn

Psalm 78 gives us just seven plagues, omitting the plagues of darkness, boils, and cattle disease. Psalm 105 also speaks of seven plagues, with "darkness" as the first, "blood" as second, "insects and lice" combined into one plague, and no plagues of either "cattle disease" or "boils." So, if you want to assert that plagues struck Egypt precisely as the Bible describes, we have to ask, were there seven or ten? Did the plagues include pestilence, lice, insects, and darkness or not? And what was the order? As for me, I turn to the bigger picture, which is this: I believe the Hebrew Bible to be true, each and every word. That is to say, the Hebrew Bible's truth is a spiritual truth, a kind of truth that is very different from every other kind of truth there is.

## Spiritual Lessons

Early twentieth-century Jewish thinker Franz Rosenzweig considers the story of the parting of the Sea of Reeds in Exodus 14–15. He writes:

> Nothing is miraculous about a miracle except that it comes when it does. The east wind has probably swept bare the ford in the Red Sea hundreds of times, and will do so again hundreds of times. But that it did this at a moment when the people in their distress set foot in the sea—that is the miracle.[5]

That's the first spiritual takeaway. As with the plagues—whether there were ten, seven, or more or fewer, regardless of which one followed the other—the miracle was in the timing, that something important happened when the people needed it to happen, just as we hope to encounter such good fortune in our lives, too, just when we need it.

So you can see that I am building the argument to support the statement that the Hebrew Bible is true. There's a spiritual and moral truth in each and every word. The Hebrew Bible's truth may not have much to do with the truth of dermatology, biology, or ecology, or the truth of history, either. The Hebrew Bible is neither a science textbook nor a history primer. The Hebrew Bible provides a spiritual basis for hope and wonder. It provides a positive message for the darkest times.

Let me say something else about miracles: I believe in miracles. For instance, I pray for miracles when I recite the *Mi Shebeirach* prayer for healing of the sick and injured, just as I also trust the healing powers of medical science, all at the same time. Inconsistent? Of course! But religion lets a person be that way, and there is no law against it. Having faith allows for, almost demands that we cherish conflicting ideas. A person can hold both faith and fact in the heart, no matter how deeply religion and nature appear to conflict.

In another moral lesson in the "ten" plagues—that's what I like to call them—that "Act of God" in ten acts affirms the importance of the "freedom from" and the "freedom to." That is to say, the freedom from slavery in Egypt speaks to the moral truth in the need for each person to possess and exercise the freedom to make personal decisions. Each person deserves the "freedom from" material want and spiritual hardship, freedom from suffering the likes of which we encountered as slaves in Egypt. A complete person enjoys the ability to exercise the "freedom to" take the Hebrew Bible's teachings to heart. Freedom is so fundamental that the Torah instructs us to forever remember the heartache of slave life and never to oppress anyone as we were oppressed. What's more, the privileged among us are responsible for giving back to those in need by working to ensure their freedom, too.

Finally, the ten plagues are also an object lesson in the need for climate protection. The story speaks to our responsibility to care for the fragile earth God placed in our trust. Devastating natural disasters and disorders—foul water, spreading disease, darkened skies, and more—afflict our planet today, just as they do in this Hebrew Bible narrative. This story calls us to continue God's work of creation by being responsible stewards of our earth.

So there are a number of truths in the story of the ten plagues and the splitting of the Sea of Reeds:

- The miracle of lifesaving help that arrives just when we need it.

- The common human yearning and need for freedom—freedom from oppression and freedom to exercise conscience.

- The call to be responsible stewards of this earth that God placed in our care.

Let's turn from the spiritual truths in the book of Exodus to a broader conversation about the spiritual truth of the Hebrew Bible.

## The Spiritual Truth of the Hebrew Bible

The Republican presidential candidates got it right when they described religious truth as "allegorical." In another example of allegory, see how the book of Psalms (23:1) offers the famous words

"The Lord is my Shepherd." No one I know comes away from that verse believing that God is literally wandering the desert carrying a shepherd's rod while the people eat scrub growth and grow fleece. "The Lord is my Shepherd" is metaphor. It's poetry. It's also poetry when the Hebrew Bible tells us that God and Moses work miracles to free us from slavery. Recognizing the Bible's truth means recognizing that the Bible's hyperbole contains a moral or spiritual lesson.

The Hebrew Bible's truth is not like the scientific truth that tells us when water freezes and boils, what the earth is made of, and how the weather comes to be. The Hebrew Bible's truth is not the historical truth that pinpoints what happened in ancient times—who, where, what, when, how, or why. The Hebrew Bible's laws are not like the modern Internal Revenue Service Tax Code, which determines whether an expense is either deductible or it isn't, leaving no middle ground. Nor is it like the Major League Baseball rulebook, which insists that every baserunner is either safe or out and that each pitch is either a ball or a strike and the plate umpire's decision is final. The Hebrew Bible's truth is not like any of that, at all.

We made two claims as this book opened. First we said that the Hebrew Bible is true and we saw the Hebrew Bible's spiritual truth in the instructions for caring for medical conditions, in considering good health as a spiritual concern, in upholding human dignity by restoring a healed person to the community, and in the lessons of "freedom from" and "freedom to." Second, as we will soon see, the Hebrew Bible wants us to tell the truth, and as we turn to the writings of the rabbis, the Mishnah, the Talmud, the Midrash, and more, we see how the Jewish value of truth evolved through the centuries, an approach that is remarkably relevant to our times. To see how the Hebrew Bible speaks today, let's turn to a contemporary example.

## Putting Spiritual Truth into Practice: A Truthful Sampler

It was a moment of historic embarrassment when the Federal Trade Commission accused the Campbell's Soup Company of deception in advertising for placing clear glass marbles at the bottom of soup bowls used in its commercials. The ploy prevented meat and vegetables from sinking out of sight and led consumers to think the soup had more solid ingredients than it really did. In response to the charges, Campbell's offered a marble-mouthed apology, pulled the commercials, and stopped lining the bottoms of its bowls.[6] A half-century later, the incident stands as a classic example of the very thing the Hebrew Bible wants us to avoid.

The Hebrew Bible and the rabbis set a high standard for truthfulness in business and in life in general. As we read earlier, the Hebrew Bible wants us to "keep far from falsehood" (Exodus 23:7) and the verse "You shall not steal, you shall not deal falsely, and you shall not lie to each other" (Leviticus 19:11) equates lying with robbery and corruption. The rabbis elaborate on, expand on, and clarify those teachings. Rabbi Hanina says, "God's seal is truth" (Talmud, *Shabbat* 55a), and the Midrash places truth among the earth's underpinnings with Rabbi Shimon ben Gamliel's words, "The world rests on three things: on justice, on truth, and on peace" (*Pirke Avot* 1:18). Again, the rabbis speak in hyperbole just as the Hebrew Bible does, as when Rabbah of the Talmud imagines that the first question on the entrance interview for heaven is, "Were you honest in your business dealings?" (*Shabbat* 31a). After all, the psalmist addresses God with these words: "You will destroy those who lie. You hate all the workers of iniquity." (Psalm 5:7). Rabbi Yermeyah ben Abba goes on to warn, "Liars cannot behold God's majesty" (Sotah 42a), and Mar, the son of Rabinah, closes his prayers with "My God, keep my tongue from evil and my lips from deceitful speech" (*Berachot* 17a).

The rabbis specifically caution their colleagues when speaking about their Jewish learning: when someone overpraises your Talmud scholarship—when they say you know the whole Talmud when you understand only a small part—it is upon the praised party to dispel the mistaken impression by saying, "I just know just one section" (Jerusalem Talmud, *Makkot* 2:6), meaning that a rabbi has an obligation to clear up a false impression, even if it reduces the rabbi's stature.[7]

Within that larger context let's return to Jewish business ethics. The Hebrew Bible insists on trustworthiness in business by calling for "honest scales, honest weights, an honest dry measure, and an honest liquid measure. I am the Eternal, your God, who brought you out of the land of Egypt" (Leviticus 19:36). The point here is that the merchant owns the scale, enjoys the upper hand at the sales counter, and should not exploit that higher position to take advantage of the buyer. The buyer has no option but to rely on the merchant's measures for accuracy, so the Hebrew Bible's regulation balances the relationship. Honesty in business is such a core Jewish value that Rashi takes that verse's reference to the redemption from Egypt to underscore that God brought us out of there "on condition that you have these honest measures."[8] Serious as the rabbis are about honest scales and honesty in speech, Rabbi Yosi ben Yehudah puns on the Hebrew words for yes, *ken*, and the Hebrew weight measure, *hin*, to say that "your *hin*" should be honest as "your *yes*" (Talmud, *Bava Metzia* 49a).

The Talmud provides another illustration by giving us the term *g'nevat da'at*, or "theft of knowledge." *G'nevat da'at* speaks to providing misinformation and/or allowing a misconception to stand. It's "theft of knowledge" to make soup appear heftier than it really is in hopes that this false presentation will lead to a purchase that would not have occurred if the customer had the facts. And the Talmud gives more than a ladle full of wisdom when literally condemning the intentional exaggeration of the value of merchandise by placing the better items at the top of a bin, thereby misleading the customer into thinking that the quality throughout is higher than it is. The prohibition against hiding the few bad apples at the bottom of the barrel extends to the prohibition against soaking meat in water to make it appear plumper or painting animals or utensils to lead a buyer to think they are younger or newer, respectively (*Bava Metzia* 60a–b). Hiding the truth is the same as lying;

failing to disclose the truth is the same as lying, too. You'll compare two cans of soup or two barrels of barley and you'll come away with a product you wouldn't have purchased had you had accurate information. A person needs the facts in order to make a sound decision.

## A Day without Lying

The Hebrew Bible is true and wants us to be truthful, and we can all agree that honesty is the best policy, but let's get real. Try going through just one day without lying—it probably would be easier to go see the movie *Liar, Liar.* In what many consider a silly comedy, a professionally successful, though personally challenged lawyer lies all the time. He tells one lie too many by lying to his son about the reason for missing the boy's birthday party. By then the son has had his fill and wishes for his birthday that Dad would tell the truth for an entire twenty-four hours—no lying at all for a full day. Well, wouldn't you know it, the wish comes true. Dad speaks his honest mind, even in some of the most awkward situations, to the dismay of other film characters and the amusement of the audience. This standard romantic comedy includes all the personal, professional, and humorous ups and downs, punctuated by Dad blurting out embarrassing things that he would have been better off keeping to himself instead of opening his unfiltered mouth to alienate coworkers, acquaintances, and friends. It doesn't take much imagination to realize that some things are best left unsaid. More to the point, you can't go through a day without telling a lie.

Even if you're not familiar with this movie, it's all too tempting to dismiss the Hebrew Bible's high moral ideals as unattainable and unrealistic. But the Hebrew Bible is realistic. It recognizes that everyone lies at one point or another. It understands that moral living calls for an ongoing balance of competing values. When life is at odds with itself, the responsibility falls to the person in the situation to consider the unique and specific circumstances at that time, come to a decision, and act on it, with the Hebrew Bible as a guide through it all.

As we close part 1, we can say that the Hebrew Bible loves the truth and wants us to love and honor the truth, too, be it the truth of science, history, or the spirit. We also know that the Hebrew Bible specializes in moral and spiritual truth, even as it recognizes the potential for moral good in a lie. Part 2 explores the Hebrew Bible's so-called "little" lies, including the "white" lies intended to spare feelings or avoid embarrassment, embellishment of the truth, half-truths, and finally paternalistic or benevolent lies. Part 3 considers "bigger" lies.

I call "little" lies "little" because they look like they're little. They appear to serve a positive purpose while causing little if any damage. What's more, the liar doesn't see much distance between the whole truth and a little lie—close enough is good enough. But, a careful inspection shows that the distance is much greater than it seems and that quick self-reassurance of moral closeness is nothing more than a self-deception that makes one lie into two. When I tell a little lie, I'm lying to myself on top of lying to you. Despite the temptation to ignore these little lies, it pays to give them a closer look.

Part II

# Little Lies

## Chapter 3

# The White Lie

### "Do I Look Big?"

A little lie makes a big difference in a recent TV commercial. President Abraham Lincoln and his wife, Mary Todd Lincoln, are getting dressed for a formal evening out. Mary Todd asks Honest Abe whether the dress she is wearing makes her look big. He squirms and fidgets, begins to speak, and you can imagine the rest.

I don't know what the real President Lincoln did in those delicate social situations—whether he said exactly what he thought or whether he chose words with an eye toward preventing hard feelings. He wasn't Jewish, of course, but he was the kind of guy who considered his words before he spoke, just as the rabbis caution when they advise, "Give thought to what comes out of your mouth" (Talmud, *Derech Eretz Zuta* 3:1). That's good advice, especially when it comes to the "white" lie.

The white lie is the letter signed, "With best personal wishes," written to someone you despise. It's the excuse "We need to head home now because the babysitter has a curfew," when the dinner party gets boring. It's the "Thank you!" note for the gift of a hideous tie you already returned to the store. It's responding to "How are you?" with "It's all good," when it's not. These are "little" lies, far from perjury, and they're told with noble, or at least benign, intentions. We take the white lie as harmless, even helpful, when it heads off hard feelings or covers over a trivial indiscretion.

We pay little attention to little lies because they are so common and seem so trivial, making the consideration of this kind of lie appear to be more like nitpicking than serious Torah study. What's more, the Hebrew Bible and the rabbis give the white lie their blessing. But the reality is that every lie, even a little one, comes at a cost, and examining the white lie crystallizes the significance and impact of all lying, big and small. Let's look the story of Sarah, Abraham, and their guests.

## "I Didn't Laugh"

Abraham and Sarah dream of being parents, but that dream has not yet come to pass as they enter old age without an heir. One day, they welcome three visitors into their tent for a meal and conversation. Sarah overhears the visitors convey the unbelievable news that she will become pregnant and bear a child in due time. Sarah could have reacted with "That's great!" and left it at that. Instead, she knows that biological parenthood is physically impossible:

> Abraham and Sarah were well up in years, and Sarah had stopped having periods. So Sarah laughed to herself, saying, "Will I have enjoyment? And my husband is old!" (Genesis 18:11–12)

Sarah laughs inside, but God hears it anyway.

> God asked Abraham, "Why did Sarah laugh like that, as if to say, 'As if I'll really give birth! I'm old!'? Is anything too wondrous for God? I will return to you at the same season and Sarah will have a son." But Sarah denied, saying, "I did not laugh," because she was afraid, but God said, "No, you laughed." (Genesis 18:13–15)

There are a few things going on here. The first has to do with the smothered laugh, which God takes as a show of disrespect, even lack of faith. The other issue is the lie itself: Sarah denies that she laughed. As for the first issue, the one of disrespect, the Midrash has God confront Sarah with "I can create a person from the beginning. I cannot restore a person's youth?" (Genesis Rabbah 48:19). In the Midrash, God accuses Sarah of near heresy to think that pregnancy at her advanced age is beyond God's ability. Yet, the physical reality is that she and her husband are "well up in years." It *would* take a miracle for her to have a child at her age, and as a pragmatic soul, Sarah knows better than to rely on miracles. Sarah is too humble to assume that God would change the course of nature just for her even with the Covenant and Jewish destiny at stake. The tension is high and the context significant, making the transgression appear so much the smaller and the miracle of birth and parenting so much more wondrous.

The commentator Rashi, reacting to the Hebrew Bible's words, "Sarah laughed to herself," offers, "She looked at herself and said, 'Will this body carry a child? These breasts are dry. Will they give milk?'"[1] As for me, I give Sarah credit for stifling her reaction instead of blurting out a belly laugh in disrespect to her guests. On top of that, the laugh is more of a startle reaction than anything else. Sarah could just as easily have cried out or shouted, the way any of us would upon hearing good news, like winning the lottery, that takes us by surprise. If you have kids, what did you do when you found out that you would be a parent?

So that is the first issue: Sarah laughs, God calls her on it, and the matter is done. As for the second, Sarah gets scared when God confronts her about the laugh. She reacts with another startle reaction, blurting out a lie: "I did not laugh." That was a white lie, a lie of denial. God could have punished Sarah for both transgressions—the disrespect and the lie. But God lets it all go by the wayside and the story continues.

While God moves on, Sarah doesn't forget. If you stifle a laugh and God calls you on it, you'd still be reeling a year later, as Sarah is. She holds onto the memory of that incident when her son is born, and she names him Isaac, *Yitzhak*—Hebrew for "He will laugh." So Sarah lies, God reprimands, but does not punish her. That white lie? Noticed and acknowledged. Now move on.

Beyond being a parent myself, I can't speak to the scientific or medical truths in the miracle of birth. But I can comment on a spiritual truth in the story of the birth of Isaac.

Sarah and Abraham are in a very serious situation without an heir. Their relationship with God and the Jewish future hang in the balance. But that isn't the only time the future of a family and the people face challenge. Taking a broader perspective of Jewish history, let's highlight the absurd and miraculous reality of the Covenant with God and Jewish continuity. Says Rabbi Samson Raphael Hirsch, "The entire beginning of the Jewish people is laughable, its history, its expectations, its hopes."[2] Jewish continuity is "laughable"—but it's no joke and not to be taken for granted. An ongoing Jewish peoplehood is as much a miracle as the miraculous arrival of Isaac.

So here we have our first lie. It is a little lie about a quiet laugh. It isn't much of a sin, and it isn't punished either. We all lie that way, but before we move on, let's look at this story through the eyes of the rabbis, who raise a question: Does God lie, too?

## Does God Lie?

God makes peace with Sarah's lie, which might lead a reader to think God doesn't worry much about that kind of lie, or any kind of lying, at all. Hard as it is to imagine God tolerating a lie, it's harder to think that God would tell one, even a small one, or even give the appearance of doing such a thing. But, as we will now see, the rabbis open the door to thinking that even God is not a faithful reporter of the truth.

The rabbis are careful students of the Hebrew Bible text; they thoughtfully weigh the Hebrew Bible's language and nuance. And when it comes to God's speaking, God never wastes a word or omits even a syllable, unless there is a good reason for God to do so.

In one Talmud passage, the rabbis call attention to the way God restates Sarah's words:

> The School of Ishmael taught: Peace is great, because even God changed something for it, as it is written, "So Sarah laughed to herself, saying, 'Will I have enjoyment? And my husband is old!'" and it is also written "God asked Abraham, 'Why did Sarah laugh like that, as if to say, "As if I'll really give birth! I'm old!"? Is anything too wondrous for God?'" (*Bava Metzia* 87a)

What a smart Hebrew Bible and what sharp rabbis!

Now I don't want to make more of this than we should, but the Hebrew Bible says, "Sarah laughed to herself, saying, 'Will I have enjoyment? And my husband is old!'" The Hebrew Bible also shows God paraphrasing Sarah as saying, "As if I'll really give birth! I'm old!" The rabbis point out that when God repeats Sarah's statement, God says nothing about Abraham's age, even though Sarah does. God shifts the focus away from Abraham onto Sarah. As the Talmud explains, "The School of Ishmael taught, "Peace is great because even the Holy One, the Blessed One, made this change" (*Bava Metzia* 87a) to safeguard Abraham's feelings and preserve the peace.

The rabbis of the Talmud take God and the Hebrew Bible as full and faithful reporters. But here, God omits part of Sarah's remarks, the part where she describes Abraham as "old." The rabbis want us to know that God decides on this omission to preserve Abraham's feelings. God knows Abraham is a very sensitive guy who needs an extra measure of emotional protection.

Sarah is too modest and too humble to be concerned or take offense about her age. So there is no harm done when God points out that she is up in years. But Abraham has a vanity about himself, and God doesn't want to hurt Abraham by reminding him that he is old. The rabbis show that God shades the language to teach that "peace is great." Peace merits a measure of protection and strengthening that comes from telling a white lie of omission.

To be sure, the Hebrew Bible and the rabbis approach aging, gender, and stigma in their own way, with an understanding that is likely very different from ours. What's more, there may not seem to be much substance or importance in this word game, but the rabbis certainly think so, to the point of making sure we know that God parses words "to preserve the peace." And in a body of Jewish literature that upholds God's conduct as our moral beacon, the rabbis lift up this example of how carefully we ought to weigh and edit our words in order to preserve the peace.

I don't think they are having a sale on white lies in this chapter of the Hebrew Bible, even though the rabbis are open to the possibility that God joins the fray. But, in all seriousness, it really is remarkable that the rabbis of the Talmud lead us to believe that God uses a lie of omission for any reason. You'd think they would want God to refrain from lying, but no. To be clear, I'm not calling God a liar on the basis of these words. The point in this story is that by invoking God's example, the Talmud invites us to consider that a lie is permissible—even advisable—in a delicate social situation. But before we run off and give ourselves permission to lie with abandon, let's turn to the rabbis for a look at another side of this kind of little lie.

## What Do You Say to the Wedding Couple? Encouraging the White Lie

Imagine you're at a wedding and you're about to talk with the groom or the bride. The Talmud asks:

> What should a person say to a bride? The School of Shammai says, "A bride as she is." But the School of Hillel says, "A beautiful and graceful bride."

The School Shammai would have us tell a bride—or a groom—exactly what we see, for better or worse. Hillel, on the other hand, expects a guest to say something positive, no matter what. The Talmud's conversation continues:

> The School of Shammai went on to question the School of Hillel: Is it proper to say that she is beautiful and graceful since the Torah says, "Keep far from falsehood" (Exodus 23:7)?

But the School of Hillel holds its ground:

> Said the School of Hillel to the School of Shammai: Think about what you are saying. If a person gets a bad deal in the marketplace, should people praise it or disparage it? Surely they should praise it.

Hillel expects a person to consider the situation and the participants' feelings before speaking, especially when it comes to "truth dumping." The Talmud agrees with Hillel and tells us:

> From this the Sages derived the rule that a person should always conduct oneself in a pleasant manner. (*Ketubot* 16b–17a)

You don't have to wonder who got more wedding invitations. But, more to the point, Shammai upholds the specific language of the Torah and the letter of the law, while Hillel seeks its spirit. Of course, Hillel knows that the Hebrew Bible teaches, "Keep far from falsehood." He doesn't need Shammai to remind him. He also recognizes the reality of lived life. He understands that none of us wants our spirits crushed at a delicate moment.

It's easy to look at that Hillel-Shammai exchange and just say, "Oh, the rabbis are a polite bunch. Go ahead and lie when you're in a tight spot. Let's get on with the wedding," and let this book move on to the next chapter. But it's much more complicated than that, and the big focus on little lies now continues. First, the rabbis favor Hillel's opinion, just as they also record Shammai's opinion for the generations, and this raises some important considerations. The Talmud takes outvoted ideas and records them all the time and, by doing so, sets a model for respectful disagreement. The Talmud preserves Shammai's rejected view out of admiration for a colleague. The Talmud also wants us to know that it cherishes learning a variety of perspectives, even perspectives it turns down. The rabbis expect us to respect our opponents, rather than wipe the floor with them.

There is another good reason to keep Shammai's words in mind, for the times a bride, a groom, or anyone else needs more than empty praise. What if you are the one getting married and want a trusted opinion about a suit or gown, the guest list, or some other detail? What if you're going on a job interview and need to know whether or not your outfit is appropriate? Shammai's insistence on the unvarnished truth calls attention to the times that "putting it all on the table" is the right thing to do, even if the truth hurts, though one of those tables is not likely to be at a wedding reception. Now, we have one more point to cover before closing this conversation on the white lie.

## Intentional or Spontaneous? The Gaffe

Sarah's laugh is an example of a gaffe, a social blunder. She wants to keep that laugh private, but she gets caught.

Some gaffes are visual—imagine a United States president photographed on the golf course during a national emergency or Costco labeling Bibles as "Fiction." Other gaffes are verbal, as in a former president admitting to a reporter that he has a lusting heart or a former vice president's misspelling of a common vegetable. Once that blooper catches the media's eye or ear, it gets amplified and played and replayed, all to the embarrassment of the gaffer.

Of course, the higher the social status of the gaffer, the more damage accrues to the gaffer's reputation, to the point of ending a career, costing a political election, or tanking a popular consumer product. Apologies, contrition, or other efforts to make amends may not silence the frenzy of unwanted attention or make the public forget. Once that gaffe gets out there, a political leader, a sports figure, or a business mogul will be willing to do just about anything to take back the gaffe, even to the point of lying.

Sarah's laugh is a verbal gaffe—unintended and impulsive, mortifying and regretted. The worst part of a gaffe like Sarah's is that it reveals her honest feelings and makes an observer conclude that she was lying about her faith all along. That is to say, a gaffe like hers casts a shadow on the previous truthfulness of the gaffer, calling all earlier statements into question. Imagine that a wedding guest who praises the bride's gown to her face later gets caught saying, "I didn't like the bride's dress at all" to her best friend, who helped pick out the dress. It's awful when the guest who compliments the groom's tux later goes on to say, "It didn't fit" in front of another guest who also happens to be the tailor.

When caught in a gaffe, the best advice I've found comes from psychologist Dan Ariely, a professor of psychology and behavioral economics at Duke University:

> Once you see that something has gone out of whack, if you recognize it, the right thing to do is to say, "You know what? Here is the mistake I made." Come up with it as soon as possible, and get it over as soon as possible. When people try to hide things they can only get worse.[3]

Sarah's gaffe of a laugh and the denial that follows is one of the many different kinds of socially awkward moments that our Hebrew Bible preserves in detail. The Hebrew Bible was the video recorder of its day, always running, including times when our spiritual ancestors were unaware. Then the rabbis enter the picture and, like a team of relentless news reporters, political pundits, and media critics, give careful scrutiny to the recorded behavior—and occasional antics—of our spiritual ancestors. The rabbis go out of their way to make sure we know what they imagine to be background information behind those "gotcha!" moments and what lessons we ought to come away with. You have to wonder if the people of the Hebrew Bible would have behaved differently had they known that the holy books would inscribe their words and deeds in detail for close analysis through the generations.

So, at the end of all this deliberation and conversation, we can all agree that a little lie about a smothered chortle or a wedding suit or dress makes a big difference, as we move from the white lie to the embellishment.

# Chapter 4

# Embellishment

If you need to lie, don't lie too much. That's another piece of advice from Professor Dan Ariely of Duke. Professor Ariely finds that people are more likely to lie about smaller things than larger ones. A person will think nothing of stealing a pad of paper from the office. But the theft of the monthly payroll goes beyond most people's sense of propriety. On a dating website a person adds an inch to his height and takes off a few pounds. But no one makes himself a foot taller or thirty pounds lighter.[1]

Of course there were no dating websites in the Garden of Eden. They didn't need any. Dating options were few, and besides, technology was limited. Nevertheless, the experience in Eden demonstrates how a little embellishment contributed to one of the biggest sins in the Hebrew Bible.

## Did God Say, "Don't Touch"?

It's only human nature to be curious about rules and what happens when they're broken, especially when it comes to kids. The more an adult forbids, the more a kid will be tempted to cross the line, if only to see what all the fuss is all about. Warning a child, "You'll catch cold going bareheaded in the winter," increases the temptation to run hatless around the schoolyard. The sign "Wet paint! Don't touch!" invites a finger smear to see for oneself. And of course, "Don't walk on the drying concrete!" advertises the opportunity to inscribe one's initials in perpetuity.

Adam and Eve, like a couple of kids without an adult in the room, break the only rule they have by eating from the Tree of Knowledge of Good and Evil.

> God commanded the man, saying, "You may eat all you like of every tree in the garden, but the Tree of Knowledge of Good and Evil you may not eat because the day you eat from it you will certainly die." (Genesis 2:16–17)

Eden is an all-you-can-eat buffet, with that fruit of the Tree of Knowledge of Good and Evil the only item not on the menu. And, with that temptation growing in the center of the Garden, Adam and Eve need just a little bit of encouragement to break the rule, and the serpent gives it to them.

> The serpent was the most cunning of all the animals God created. It said to the woman, "Did God really say, 'You may not eat of any tree in the Garden'?" The woman said to the serpent, "Of any tree in the Garden we may eat the fruit, and God said, 'But, the fruit of the tree in the middle of the Garden, do not eat it, and do not even touch it, or you will die.'" The serpent said to the woman, "You will certainly not die because God knows that on the day that you do eat of it, your eyes will be opened and you will be like God, knowing good from evil." (Genesis 3:1–5)

The invitation is in the tree's very name: "the Tree of Knowledge of Good and Evil," as if to say, "Have a bite and you'll get real smart." Who wouldn't want to become a "know-it-all"?

As for the punishment of death, the more serious the warning, the easier it becomes to brush it off, which explains how "you will certainly die" evokes the equivalent of a yawn and, "Oh, yeah. Sure!" as if to say, "God wouldn't do *that!*"

More to the point, let's look at how "Don't eat" morphs into "Don't touch." The Hebrew Bible doesn't explain what brings about that embellishment. Maybe Adam isn't paying attention when God gives him instructions. Maybe Adam adds a little of his own spin to God's warning, to keep Eve far away from the tree and trouble. Maybe Eve makes it up on her own.

The rabbis tend to blame Eve, with the serpent in a supporting, instigating role. Rashi explains that her embellishment contributes to the sin of eating:

> *Do not even touch it*: She added to the command, thereby weakening it.[2]

Thanks to Eve, more becomes less.

The serpent recognizes that Eve is gullible. Also from Rashi:

> *When the woman saw* the *tree was good for food*: The words of the serpent appealed to her and pleased her, so she believed him.[3]

In contrast to Rashi, the Midrash heaps as much blame as possible on the serpent, starting by casting the beast as a brute:

> When the serpent saw her passing by the tree, he took her and threw her against it. He said to her, "See, you didn't die. Just as you didn't die from touching it, you will not die by eating it." (*Genesis Rabbah* 19:3)

But back to Rashi, who views the serpent as less of a bully and more of a smooth talker:

> *You shall not eat of every tree in the garden*: Though the serpent saw them eating other fruits, he got into a long conversation with her and led the topic to that tree.[4]

So, take your choice, whether the serpent is guilty of rough behavior and/or playing fast and loose with the truth. Regardless, embellishment of the truth contributes to eating the fruit and the resulting sin and punishment. The moral: Stick to the story. Exaggeration opens the door to trouble, and trouble is exactly what walked in.

## Where Was Adam?

Now the rabbis wonder, "Where is Adam when the serpent pushes Eve around or bends her ear? Why is he missing in action?"

For all we read about Adam in the Hebrew Bible, we know very little about him. He doesn't have much of a personality or much willfulness. God decides that Adam should not be alone and creates Eve, Adam's partner and soul mate. God doesn't ask Adam, and Adam isn't complaining that he needs a companion—God decides on Adam's behalf. Adam takes no active part in Eve's creation; what's more, he sleeps through the whole thing and has no reaction when she appears on the scene. And, when she suggests that he taste the fruit, he simply goes ahead and bites into it. So there doesn't seem to be much to Adam; he's a pretty passive guy. This brings us back to our question. Just what is Adam up to when the serpent flexes its muscles or works its charm?

Some rabbis defend Adam's absence, saying he is on the job.

God took him and led him all around the world, telling him, "Here is a place for planting trees, here is a place for planting seeds." (*Genesis Rabbah* 19:3)

God assigns him and Eve the task of caring for the earth. He is following God's instructions for planet care when the serpent is talking up Eve (Genesis 1:28).

In another opinion, Abba bar Kuriah says, "He [Adam] had intercourse and then fell asleep" (*Genesis Rabbah* 19:3). But before branding Adam as self-absorbed or lazy, let's remember that God commands the first human beings to "be fruitful and multiply"

(Genesis 1:28), meaning Adam and Eve are fulfilling their responsibilities. This raises an interesting possibility that flies in the face of some religious beliefs: Adam and Even had sex in Eden, even before the expulsion. Either way, tending to the Garden or having had sex, Adam was honoring God.

## Born in Eden

The Hebrew Bible's tales often resemble those Rudyard Kipling "Just So Stories," told to explain "How the Camel Got His Hump," "How the Leopard Got His Spots," and the like. You could say that the Hebrew Bible's record of events in the Garden of Eden is a weaving together of "Just So Stories" that show how the snake lost its legs, why work is so frustrating, why childbirth is so painful, and more. Many religious interpreters have taken the story of the "fall" from Eden to also explain how sex came to be. These teachers say that sex is a consequence of eating the forbidden fruit, in a bundle of sin, guilt, and punishment. That is to say, they are convinced that sex begins with sin and that sex retains some of that sin today, but this line of thought conflicts with the Jewish teaching that says Adam and Eve were intimate in Eden, even before the expulsion.

Rashi looks closely at the Hebrew Bible text, describing the birth of Adam and Eve's first child, Cain, and concludes that Eve became pregnant in Eden:

> *The man knew Eve, his wife. She got pregnant and delivered Cain*: This was before the above-mentioned incident, before the sin and the expulsion from Eden, that is to say, the pregnancy and the delivery.[5]

Rashi goes on to point out that the grammar of Genesis 4:1 indicates that Cain is born in Eden and that sex has nothing at all to do with disobeying God's one and only restriction. There is sex in Eden from the very start, meaning that sexual intimacy has less to do with human sinfulness and is more about God's grace; that is, sex is part of how God made us. So, if you want an example of an important difference between Jewish teachings and the teachings of other faiths, go back to where the Hebrew Bible began and when people came to be.

As we study Jewish thinking through the centuries, we see that Judaism has long taught that sex is not inherently sinful, but potentially holy when strengthening the bonds in a committed relationship. Sex has nothing to do with the Tree of Knowledge of Good and Evil. "Just so," it was there from the very start.

Returning to the story, no matter where Adam is during that fateful conversation, how the serpent treats or mistreats Eve, or how we get from eating to touching, God punishes all involved, sentencing Adam to a life of toil, Eve to the pain of childbirth and living under her husband's domination, and the serpent to a diet of dirt and misery. Our focus on lying, however, brings us to back to the embellishment, the expansion of "Don't eat" into "Don't touch" that leads to Adam and Eve getting the boot and making Eden their home no more. However, the "fall from Eden" changes the course of human destiny for the better; Judaism sees a positive outcome from this story, and we will return to see what this means when we build that framework for discernment.

## When Lying Resembles the Truth

Bad things happen when lying resembles the truth, as when "Don't eat" becomes "Don't touch." The rabbis well understand the dangers in rhetorical distortion, as when the serpent duped Eve and Pharaoh enslaved the people of Israel.

As we are beginning to see, the rabbis often spin Hebrew puns to draw out an idea from the Hebrew Bible. The rabbis point out that Pharaoh enslaves us *b'farech*, in Hebrew, literally "with bitterness," resembling another Hebrew phrase, *b'fe rach*, "with a smooth mouth." That is to say, Pharaoh relies on "slick speech" or "gentle persuasion" to entrap us (*Exodus Rabbah* 1:11). The rabbis underscore how careful wordsmithing has furthered many a malevolent agenda, as in Pharaoh's era, in their own time, as well as in our day.

TV personality Stephen Colbert coined the term "truthiness" to explain what's "tearing our country apart":

> It used to be, everyone was entitled to their own opinion, but not their own facts. But that's not the case anymore. Facts matter not at all. Perception is everything.... What is important? What you want to be true, or what *is* true?... Truthiness is "What I say is right, and [nothing] anyone else says could possibly be true." It's not only that I *feel* it to be true, but that *I* feel it to be true. There's not only an emotional quality, but there's a selfish quality.[6]

If it sounds true to me, that's all I need to know.

Charles Siefe, a journalism professor at New York University, put forward the term "proofiness" to show how "people exploit numbers to make things sound reasonable."[7] He looked back to the 1950s and the hearings of the Un-American Activities Committee of the United States House of Representatives, devoted to disclosing and eradicating communism in the United States during the Cold War. Proofiness means that if it sounds true and looks true then it must be true.

> As he held aloft a sheaf of papers, a beetle-browed [Senator] Joe McCarthy assured his place in the history books with his bold claim: "I have here in my hand a list of 205—a list of names that were made known to the Secretary of State as being members of the Communist party and who nevertheless are still working and shaping policy in the State Department."
>
> That number—205—was a jolt of electricity that shocked Washington into action against communist infiltrators.

Never mind that the number was a fabrication. The number went up to 207 and then dropped down again the following day, when McCarthy wrote to President [Harry S.] Truman claiming that "we have been able to compile a list of 57 Communists in the State Department." A few days later, the number stabilized at 81 "security risks." McCarthy gave a lengthy speech in the Senate, giving some details about a large number of cases (fewer than 81, in fact) but without revealing enough information for others to check into the matter.

It really didn't matter whether the list had 205 or 57 or 81 names. The very fact that McCarthy had attached a number to his accusations imbued them with an aura of truth.[8]

So a little lie does much damage, whether the facts are watered down or cooked up. For now, having seen two kinds of little lies in the Torah—the white lie and the embellishment—we turn to the half-truth. As surely as two half-truths don't add up to a whole one, half a lie can do as much damage as a lie that's full size.

## Chapter 5

# The Half-Truth

When I'm hungry, "half a loaf is better than none," as the old saying goes. But it's an entirely different story when we get to the half-truth because half of the truth is as bad as a full-blown lie.

A half-truth is a planned and limited disclosure, intentionally revealing just enough to mislead. It exploits the truth to distract. It's an evasion, a "Watch my other hand" trick that takes advantage of something truthful to draw attention away from what isn't. We have half-truths in the Hebrew Bible, with the first one, remarkably, encouraged by God.

## "Let Us Please Go on a Three-Day Journey"

God appoints Moses to lead the people of Israel from slavery to freedom, with these words from the Hebrew Bible itself:

> Go with the elders of Israel to the king of Egypt and say to him, "The God of the Hebrews appeared to us so now, let us please go on a three-day journey in the wilderness so we may worship our God." (Exodus 3:18)

As much as the God of the Hebrews wants the slaves freed, God also wants more than a three-day wilderness excursion—God wants full and permanent freedom. This isn't a translation problem. It's exactly what the Hebrew Bible says. God sits Moses down for a conversation, and making a three-day request is exactly what the Hebrew Bible reports God telling Moses to do. God specifically instructs Moses to use language that leaves open the possibility of return, when no return is in the plans. This wordplay conceals God's full agenda while telling only half the story.

Abravanel bluntly questions God's cagey way of speaking, asking, "Why did God tell Moses to lie in God's name? Wouldn't it have been much better for Moses to say plainly, 'Free My people from the burdens of Egypt?'"[1]

It's as if Abravanel was saying to God, "Hey, why weren't You honest?" As always, there's another opinion. Hizkuni considers the words "a three-day journey" and maintains that this isn't a lie, saying, "That's just what they actually did, as it is written, 'They camped at Etham on the second day at the edge of the wilderness.'"[2]

They walk for three days and they stop; nothing misrepresented. But we know that God wants more than a desert sand-dune adventure tour. It's hard to believe that the God of truth, the God of the Hebrew Bible, tells Moses to parse his words like that.

As if God needs defenders, other commentators rush to God's defense, saying that God has a good reason for understating the end goal. Nehama Leibowitz points to Isaac Arama's midrash, *Akedat Yitzhak*, to say that it was God's plan to demonstrate Pharaoh's deep stubbornness and justify the ten plagues beyond all doubt.[3]

God has bigger worries than the moral fine points of a spoken song and verbal dance in the court of an enemy king. God is building a justification for imposing the serious hardship of the ten plagues. The three-day ploy demonstrates, for all to see, that Pharaoh is so unreasonable that he even refuses a release for an extended weekend. Having rejected the modest request, imagine what he would have said to the full request for permanent leave-taking. For now, however, let's note that God, the Hebrew Bible's God of truth, encourages a half-lie to advance a higher goal.

## "Rachel Stole Her Father's Teraphim"

What would you do if your kid left for college without saying good-bye?

Jacob and his household are living with his father-in-law, Laban, in Padan Aram, far away from Jacob's homeland, Canaan, when God tells Jacob to leave and return home. Jacob wants to follow God's instructions and go back to the Promised Land, but he is convinced that Laban will present him with an ultimatum, forcing Jacob to choose between traveling home at God's request, at the cost of leaving his family behind, or disobeying God and staying with Laban in order to continue to be with his loved ones. To avoid a confrontation and a very bad ending, Jacob and his family sneak off without a word of farewell to Laban— talk about failure to disclose! What's more, another act of lying in this story—one by Rachel—amplifies this chapter's theme of half-truths.

As Jacob and his family are preparing to take flight, the Hebrew Bible states:

> While Laban had gone to shear his sheep, Rachel stole her father's teraphim [his household idols]. On top of that, Jacob had deceived Laban the Aramean by not telling him that he was fleeing from him. (Genesis 31:19–20)

What is Laban doing with idols? What does Rachel think she is going to do with them? And why does she steal them? But first let's talk about matriarchs and patriarchs acting like kids sneaking off to a party that a parent forbids. The Hebrew Bible tells us that

> Jacob fled with everything he owned, going up, crossing the Euphrates River, and heading toward the hills of Gilead. Three days later, someone told Laban that Jacob fled, so Laban took his family with him and pursued Jacob for

seven days, until catching up with him in the hills of Gilead.
(Genesis 31:21–23)

As if there weren't enough questions already, let's ask one more:
Why does it take Laban three whole days to realize that his kids
are gone? The reality is that family talk was different back then.
With cell phones and text messaging today, we keep close tabs on
our kids, so that absence of communication would certainly seem
strange in our time. But, in the days before handheld electronics,
the nomadic lifestyle meant families needed to spread across the
arid wilderness to avoid competition for scarce grazing and water.
So, given the lack of proximity and the lack of timely communication, we can't fault Laban for the three days it takes for him to learn
that his family has set off for Canaan.

Now for our other questions. The Hebrew Bible casually mentions that Rachel steals Laban's household idols, as if expecting us
to shrug it off with "Oh, yeah. He has idols. No big deal." But we
know idolatry is a sin, and the Hebrew Bible's people believe in the
one invisible God, a God who forbids idol worship, and that is that,
right? But, when we turn to archeology and the like, idol worship
doesn't suddenly end all at once, and it wasn't unusual in biblical
times for families to keep an idol or two in the house. So Laban
has idols, but we are left with other questions, like these: Why does
Rachel steal them? Is she an idolater, too?

The rabbis of the Talmud weren't archeologists, and they
would have quickly rejected the suggestion that Judaism evolved
from idolatry to monotheism over a period of time. What's more,
they liked to hold up our ancestors as entirely faithful. Since the
rabbis had little respect for Laban, they were all too happy to imagine Laban praying to rocks. On the other hand, they loved Rachel
and refused to tolerate any negative speculation about her, leaving
them with some explaining to do.

Rashi responds to the Hebrew Bible's "Rachel had taken the
teraphim" by offering an honorable motive for the theft: "She

intended for her father to stop idol worship."[4] Rachel "stole" the idols the way a kid might "steal" a parent's cigarettes to bring an end to a bad habit. Now, let's revisit Laban's reaction to the news that his family has left, and, I promise, we'll eventually get to the lie.

It takes a full week for Laban to catch up with the family entourage. On the way, though, God speaks to Laban in a dream and warns, "Watch yourself when you speak to Jacob, good or bad" (Genesis 31:24). And when they all meet up after a seven-day chase, Laban keeps the caution in mind as he confronts Jacob with these words:

> "What did you do, stealing my heart, driving my daughters away like war captives? Why did you deceive me by sneaking away without telling me? I would have been happy to send you off with song, drum, and harp! You didn't even give me a chance to kiss my sons and daughters. Now, how foolish you look!" (Genesis 31:26–28)

I have to feel sorry for Laban, especially once he finds the character and self-restraint to lay out his grievances with such dignity. Plus, he has good reason to worry. Travel in the ancient Near East was nothing like travel as we know it today. It meant facing the very real possibility of dying from a variety of dangers, including an attack by wild animals, threats of roadside robbers, or sudden extreme weather; even a sprained ankle could be a death sentence. Laban has plenty to be upset about as he continues to vent to Jacob:

> "It is well within my power to hurt you, but the God of your ancestors said to me last night, 'Watch yourself when you speak to Jacob, good or bad.'" (Genesis 31:29)

Laban is understandably furious about the covert leave-taking and might have been justified in killing Jacob right there. But Laban takes God's words to heart and holds back.

Jacob responds by saying that he fears Laban will insist that his daughters remain in Padan Aram, leaving Jacob in an awful situation, forced to decide between following God's command and returning to Canaan—alone—or defying God and staying in Padan Aram with Laban and the family.

Laban has nothing else to say about the abandonment, yet there remains a score for him to settle over the teraphim. Laban continues speaking to Jacob, saying, "Now, then, you have gone away because you yearn so longingly for your father's house. So why did you steal my gods?" (Genesis 31:30).

Jacob promises to make good on the idol theft:

> "The person who has your gods shall not live. In front of your relatives, see for yourself what of yours I have with me and take it yourself." But Jacob did not know that Rachel had stolen them. (Genesis 31:32)

And Jacob, without all the information he needs to make an informed decision, leaves himself at risk of having to fulfill an awful promise.

Laban takes Jacob at his word, and sets out to look for the idols himself, searching from tent to tent. Meanwhile,

> Rachel had taken the idols and put them in the camel bag, sitting on them while Laban searched the tent without finding anything. She told her father, "Do not be angry, my sir, but I cannot get up for you because the way of women is with me." So he searched, but did not find the idols. (Genesis 31:34–35)

Rachel gives a good reason for not getting up, but that is only a half-truth at best. She steals the teraphim, she hides them, she knows where they are, and even though she knows her father wants them, she lets him go on a wild goose chase without saying a word. At the very least, Rachel is guilty of withholding information about stolen goods, whether or not she stole them for her father's sake.

The book of Leviticus teaches, "You shall not steal, you shall not act deceitfully or lie to each other" (19:11). Rachel breaks two rules—maybe even three—in a trifecta of stealing, deceit, and possible lying. She steals her father's idols, she hides them in the camel bag, and she doesn't own up to any of it. Meanwhile, Jacob unwisely and impulsively misspeaks by promising to impose punishment for a theft without having all the information he needs to properly address the situation. So there we have a half-lie, a half-truth, and a caravan's worth of moral complications. In reflecting on the half-truth itself, the truthful part doesn't compensate for the missing portion when the omission makes all the difference. Rachel's half-truth adds up to a full lie. As for half-truths in our own lives, it's certainly reassuring to think, "Almost everything I said was true," yet a confession like that, of morally questionable ellipsis that discloses part of the story and leaves out the rest, is a half-truth that adds up to a total lie.

## The Double Effect

Almost everything we do, lies included, cause what has been called a "double effect." A "double effect" means that an act brings on more than one consequence. Thinking big here, there's a double effect when a nation launches a preemptive airstrike against an enemy base and the attack also inflicts "collateral damage" by harming noncombatants—civilians—in the area. In another example, two patients, near death, need a new organ—say, a heart—and none is to be found. All of a sudden, another person dies in an accident, making a heart available, but the heart can save just one person, leaving the other to die, another double effect. No one intended to hurt the civilians, and no one wants to see a heart patient die. These secondary consequences, known as double effects, are unwanted outcomes of other actions.

We find double effects in the less dramatic day in, day out events of life, as when we serve one good while unavoidably undermining another. In a lighter example, a person wanting to follow the folk medicine advice to "starve a cold and feed a fever"—or is it "feed a cold and starve a fever"?—faces a dilemma when suffering from both at the same time, with something gained and something else lost, whichever version gets followed. A desired result accompanied by another consequence—like a side effect of a medication—brings us to the double effect.

We see the double effect in the Hebrew Bible, when a lie protects or advances Jewish continuity, as when Sarah denies laughing, Moses and Aaron speak only of a three-day journey, and Rachel isn't fully honest about the idols. Each of those lies safeguards the well-being of a spiritual ancestor and ensures the physical continuity of the individual and the people, each lie serving a higher purpose by making a positive contribution to the growth and destiny of the nation. As we approach our Hebrew Bible–based framework for weighing truth and falsehood, we are beginning to see the need to consider all the potential consequences of our behavior—those that are intended and those that are unanticipated or unwanted.

The benevolent or paternalistic lies in the next chapter also create double effects. The lies are told with the highest intentions, and even though they appear to be helpful, they have the potential to do more harm than good.

# Chapter 6

# The Benevolent/ Paternalistic Lie

Jacob Heym is the main character of the novel and twice-turned film *Jacob the Liar*. Jacob's story varies from book to movie to movie, but we can say that Jacob lives in the Jewish ghetto in Lodz, Poland, during the Nazi occupation of World War II. One evening, a Nazi police officer brings Jacob down to the station on a false accusation of violating the 8:00 p.m. curfew for Jews. While at the station, Jacob is stunned to overhear a radio news report of the approaching Russian army, raising Jacob's hope that World War II will soon end and the Jews will be free from Nazi rule. In a second surprise, Jacob becomes the first Jew ever released from the station alive. As a result of these two events—the overheard broadcast and his release from custody—Jacob leaves the station filled with hope.

Soon after, Jacob dissuades a friend, Mischa, from stealing potatoes—a serious crime—by sharing word of the exciting news of the approaching Russians. Knowing no one will believe that a Jew left the police station alive and unharmed, Jacob tells Mischa that he heard about the Russians on his hidden radio—it was against the law to have a radio—in a lie that is more believable than the truth. An elated Mischa agrees to keep everything Jacob says a secret. But Mischa breaks his promise to Jacob and soon the entire ghetto knows all about the approaching Russians and Jacob's "hidden radio."

In time, the desperate ghetto residents badger Jacob for even more news, but Jacob has none, so he starts making up stories to maintain the ruse and sustain hope that lifts people from despair and prevent suicides. Eventually, living that lie becomes so stressful that Jacob tells yet another lie, that his radio has stopped working, but no one believes him. After all, times are desperate and ghetto Jews want to know the exact moment when their misery will finally end. The Nazis eventually hear about this imaginary radio and set off on a destructive hunt that leads nowhere. The story has an unhappy ending—or endings, depending on which version you follow—but the question remains: Is Jacob's lie justified? It tamps down despair, bolsters hope, and protects life, all the while raising moral questions that place Jacob in grave danger.

Such extreme circumstances are fortunately rare, yet we face situations—a medical decision, a business crisis, or a family concern—that prompt similar considerations. All are very far removed from a collective crisis, like the Holocaust, yet each calls for the same kind of careful thinking that confronts our character, Jacob.

Jacob's lie is "benevolent" and "paternalistic"—"benevolent" because it appears to have served the well-being of others while putting the liar at risk and "paternalistic" because the liar single-handedly takes on the responsibility to know better than the victims of the lie. For instance, imagine I tell you, "I am going to lie to you in a minute, but don't worry. I am lying to protect you. You'll benefit from my lie." Your response? "Don't do me any favors. Hit me with the truth." Nevertheless, we tell benevolent lies all the time.

"This shot won't hurt a bit," says the nurse to the crying child. But what happens when the shot does hurt? And what will the child make of the nurse at the next visit? What else could the nurse possibly say or do to get the child to cooperate? A benevolent lie to a kid—"Stay away from the edge of the cliff. There's a monster right under it"—may protect a child from falling. But while keeping that young life safe and far from the brink is certainly all to the good, that lie will leave a parent at a loss that very evening over worries about that same monster lurking under the bed or in the corner closet.

It's easy to rationalize lying to a child by thinking, "It's for her own good." After all, who has the time to explain the details of every dangerous situation to a kid who is not going to listen or won't understand? Let's turn to what may well be lies of paternalistic benevolence in the Hebrew Bible's story of the Binding of Isaac.

## The Binding of Isaac

The Binding of Isaac is pretty straightforward, a couple dozen verses about a father and a son on a hike, and a few words from God. Nevertheless, it is one of the most complicated and puzzling narratives in the entire Hebrew Bible. The chapter before the Binding tells about the birth of Isaac, the fulfillment of God's promise that Abraham and Sarah will have a child (Genesis 21). In the Binding narrative itself, God asks Abraham to upend that blessing by sacrificing that same child as a sign of faith. Abraham goes along with the request, until the very last moment when God's angel suddenly appears to call the whole thing off, leaving plenty of questions, double effects, and attempts to address them. The rabbis take the Binding so seriously that they assign it for the Rosh Hashanah morning Torah reading. They also subject it to the same scrutiny as the rest of the Hebrew Bible, to the point of being critical of Abraham and even God.

The rabbis agree that God "tests" Abraham's faith, just as the Hebrew Bible says (Genesis 22:1), and Abraham trusts God above all else, so much so that Abraham is prepared to offer up his most precious possession, his beloved son, as God requests. The first takeaway from the story: Abraham gets a passing score on this test of faith. The Binding also repudiates child sacrifice, a popular though heinous religious practice in some quarters long ago. But what are we to make of this story in our own time?

We don't have child sacrifice anymore, though many point out that we "sacrifice" children to parents' personal or professional goals. That makes the Binding into a lesson about adult responsibility for the well-being of children—the responsibility to spend time with them, to show them they are loved, to care for them, and to make them a priority. As for our theme of lying in the Hebrew Bible, Abraham may have lied in this story—three lies of benevolent paternalism—just as God may have lied, too.

## "We Will Both Return": Half-Truth/Half-Lie

The morning after the request from God, Abraham, Isaac, and their young servants set off on the three-day journey to Mount Moriah. They arrive at the mountainside, and as Abraham and Isaac are about to head up, the Hebrew Bible states:

> Abraham said to his young servants, "Stay here with the ass. The boy and I will go there, we'll pray and both return to you." (Genesis 22:5)

Oh? We'll *both* return"? As if they're just going to climb to the top, mutter a few quick prayers, take in the fresh mountain air, and then come back, the both of them? Isn't Abraham going to sacrifice Isaac and walk down alone? Is this a lie or is it a prophecy?

Rashi responds to these questions by telling us that Abraham foresees the end at the beginning. Abraham knows they would "both return,"[1] encouraging us to take Abraham's words to the servants as a truthful prediction. Is Rashi correct that Abraham has the foresight to know the end of the story before it is over? Or does Abraham lie to the young servants and his son by failing to tell them that a sacrifice is on the agenda, whether or not Abraham carries it through to the awful end? What would they have done if Abraham had told them the truth? The text doesn't address the questions.

## "God Will See to the Lamb"

Father and son are already climbing when Isaac finally wonders aloud:

> "Here are the firestone and the wood. Where is the lamb
> for the burnt offering?" Abraham said, "God will see to the
> lamb for the burnt offering, my son." And the two of them
> went on together. (Genesis 22:7–8)

As if to say, "Where's the beef?" It turns out that God provides a
"ram," not a "lamb," close enough for a city boy like me, a sacrificial
animal all the same. In any event, how does Abraham know that
God will "see to" there being something to offer up? Again, is Abraham prophesying or is he lying because he doesn't want to be honest with his son? According to Rashi, Isaac accepts the response:

> *Both of them went together*: Abraham, who knew he was
> going to slay his son, walked along with willingness and joy,
> like Isaac, who had no idea of the matter.[2]

They march onward and upward, Abraham determined and Isaac
in ignorance.

So far, a reader can come away from this text thinking that
Abraham may have lied to his servants and his son. As we consider
the next point, we see that he may have lied by omission to his wife.

## He Doesn't Tell Sarah

You'd think a husband would tell his wife about something as
important as the well-being of their child or a word from God. That
should be especially true in the case of Sarah and Abraham. After
all, think of what she experiences with him—leaving her homeland
to travel to an unknown destination at the word of an invisible
God, going into captivity during the famines, and more. Sarah is
a devoted life partner, whose dedication to Abraham and his ideals and vision go well beyond loyalty and trust. Abraham owes her

big-time. Yet, when it comes to Abraham putting their son at risk
during the Binding, he doesn't say a word to Sarah, as if he thinks
he can get away with hiding the whole story from her. Sarah gets
no mention in the story. We only hear about her after the incident
is over, when we learn that she dies. Rashi tells us:

> The narrative of the death of Sarah follows immediately
> after the Binding of Isaac because hearing of the Binding,
> that her son had been made ready for sacrifice and had
> almost been sacrificed, came as a great shock. Her soul left
> her and she died.[3]

There's no telling what Sarah would have done had she known the
truth beforehand, though we do know that the news killed her.

## Does God Backtrack? "Put Him Up There, but Don't Harm Him"

Again, the rabbis believe that God's word is eternal—God doesn't
take anything back. So how could God ask Abraham to offer up
his son and then say, "Never mind"? Rashi also considers the possibility of double-talk from an otherwise up front and candid God.
Rashi describes Abraham confronting God about backpedaling:

> *Because now I know*: Rabbi Aba said, "Abraham said to God,
> 'Let me lay out my complaint to You. Previously, You told
> me that "through Isaac your descendants will be called."
> Then You came back and told me, "Take your son." Now
> You tell me, "Do not lay a hand upon the boy."' The Holy,
> Blessed One said to him, 'I will not violate My Covenant,
> nor will I change what came from My lips. When I told you,
> "Take your son," I am not changing what I say, that is, My
> promise that you would have descendants through Isaac. I
> did not tell you, "Kill him," but "Bring him up to the moun-
> tain." You brought him up. Take him down.'"[4]

Rashi wants us to know that God stays on one message and that Abraham mishears. The communication error is Abraham's, not God's. Again, a Hebrew "play on words." The Hebrew letter root *alef, lamed,* and *hey* can be conjugated to mean "offer Isaac as a sacrifice" or "bring Isaac up the mountain." According to this midrash, Abraham mistakes God's words as a request to kill the boy, as if God says to Abraham, "You weren't listening to me. I didn't ask you for a child sacrifice! I just said take him up the mountain! Next time, pay better attention." In the world of the rabbis, where the assumption is that God speaks clearly and only once, there is no such thing as a walk-back. But some will come away from Rashi's opinion and claim that God did a turnaround.

In the Hebrew Bible's bigger picture of truth and falsehood, the Binding gives us four incidents that raise four questions. The indefinite language of the Binding situations merely raises the possibility that Abraham lies to his servants, his son, and his wife, and what's more, God lies, too. The first three lies appear to be paternalistic and benevolent lies, intended to protect the feelings of others, and, in a double effect, also enable Abraham to avoid taking responsibility for his decisions and behaviors.

## Lying to Children

A father tells his son that "God will provide," without any idea whether God will or not. The rabbis warn against a brush-off like that:

> Rabbi Zera said, "Do not say to a child, 'I will give you something,' and then not give it, because this will teach a child to lie." (Talmud, *Sukkot* 46b)

Kids learn by watching as much as they learn by listening, meaning that adults have to be especially careful when children are around. With all the adult modeling and child learning going on, there's a need for extra caution, out of concern that a misstep will leave a child with a lifelong bad impression.

## The Cost of Paternalistic and Benevolent Lying

A friend asks for a job at the company where you work, and past personal experience with this friend makes you think better of responding with "You're hired!" So, you make up some story about there being no openings or that the previously listed job is now filled. After all, you worry that being honest and saying, "I don't think you'd be a good fit," would cause hurt feelings and damage the relationship. Or, a suitor proposes marriage, and marrying that person is the last thing you would want to do. So you make up some story about not being the marrying type. After all, why make a decent person feel bad? But each of these lies comes at a price. Writes Sissela Bok:

> Even if an open rejection does take place—as when an applicant is denied work, a request for money is turned down, an offer of marriage refused—paternalistic lies may be told to conceal the real reasons for the rejection, to retain the civility of the interaction, and to soften the blow to the self-respect of the rejected. It is … easier to say that there is no market for a writer's proposed book than that it is unreadable; or that there is no opening for a job seeker than that he lacks the necessary skills.[5]

Benevolent lies appear to protect delicate feelings and important relationships, and they may well accomplish some of that. But, on closer examination, there's little benevolence in leaving an innocent person clueless and directionless, a person whose question shows that she trusts you. A friend seeking a loan won't learn of the need to improve those business skills and the writer won't do anything to improve the manuscript, all because of your unsubstantiated assumption that telling the truth would do more damage than telling a lie. A benevolent, paternalistic lie appears to protect the listener's feelings, but not necessarily. There's a double effect in a lie that does more to protect the teller from having to voice difficult sentiments than it does to protect anyone else. Little lies bring mixed blessings.

## What Makes Lies Little

Before we move from little lies to big ones, let's pause to take stock. As we said, little lies are "little" because they contain an element of truth, or they so resemble the truth that they allow the teller to minimize the significance of a lie by saying to him- or herself that it "looks close enough to pass." There's typically an element of self-deception in this kind of little lie.

So, a lie about how a groom or bride looks at a wedding is told to keep the listener from feeling bad. It also protects the speaker from an embarrassing situation or an argument. Let's say that Abraham—not the Abraham of the Hebrew Bible but Abraham of the commercial, that is, Abe, the president—said to Mary Todd—or had Mary Todd said to Abe if he asked the question—"That dress, that suit makes you look great!" when it didn't. He might well have spared her feelings and tamped down an argument, but she would not have known whether or not she was looking her best on the ballroom floor.

Little lies exact a toll, and though the Hebrew Bible allows little lies from time to time, it's nevertheless important to be honest about this kind of lying. Honesty about lying is as important as telling the truth itself. Let's take the next chapter to acknowledge that each lie makes a difference, no matter the size, the liar's intention, or the outcome.

Little lies have an impact, as we saw in Sarah's white lie, Eve's embellishment, Abraham's benevolent paternalism, in the half-truths from Moses and Rachel, and when God instructs Moses to lie. So, before turning from little lies to big ones, let's take a few steps back to gain a broader perspective.

## Chapter 7

# Little Lies, Big Headaches

## What Do You Put in a Letter of Recommendation?

Let's say I've agreed to write a letter of recommendation for a student applying for admission to a very competitive college. I'm a rabbi and I write these letters all the time. Here, I'm convinced that I have a highly qualified applicant. I know that only a small percentage of applicants make the cut. I also assume that other sponsors think that their kids are better than everyone else and will surely exaggerate to ensure fair treatment in a competitive field overflowing with overstatements. With five, ten, or more applications for every opening and so many applicants so very special in the eyes of their sponsors, how can a top-notch candidate stand out? So I'm tempted to overstate, if only by just a little, to neutralize the other exaggerations and ensure that my applicant gets a fair shot.

Writing a letter of recommendation of no more than a page raises enough moral questions to fill a book. After all, this letter affects my candidate and competing applicants. It also reflects on me, influences my reader, and in some small way, leaves an impression on the entire application process.

## What If the Reader Discovers My Lie?

I imagine a screener sitting down to a pile of recommendations and sighing in anticipation of having to figure out what's true and what's an omission, embellishment, or half-truth written with benevolent intent. It's a good bet to assume that a seasoned admissions officer, who has read many more letters than I will ever read or write, will see through any falsehood. So it makes sense to begin by asking, "What if the reader discovers my lie?"

Bad things happen when a lie is discovered: A letter shot through with exaggerations can damage a candidate's prospects and tarnish my reputation. While I'd be devastated if my misjudgment hurt my candidate, I wouldn't be concerned about preserving my good name were I dealing with a large university or a summer camp in another state where I'd never go. But, when it comes to letters of recommendation for a local high school scholarship or community youth program, where I am known to others, a discovered exaggeration will cast a shadow on my reputation and raise a problem next time, when I am asked to write another letter for another candidate in the future. Why should a screener ever take me at my word?

Look what happened in that old Aesop's fable "The Boy Who Cried Wolf," about that young man who repeatedly tricked his neighbors into thinking a wolf was attacking his flock. The boy played this ploy so often and so well that he used up his chits, so when a wolf really did attack, none of the townsfolk paid any attention. The Talmud must have had a similar story in mind when it taught, "That is the liar's punishment. Even when telling the truth, no one pays any attention" (*Shabbat* 89b). A lie—every lie—has a cost. The boy who cried wolf, once caught in a lie, is never trusted again. He should have asked, "What if?" That is, "What if I call on people when I don't need them? What will happen to me when there's a real problem?" When considering an exaggeration in a letter of recommendation, it makes sense to ask, "What if my embellishment is recognized?" That may be enough to keep me honest.

What's more, when we consider little lies in general, it pays to acknowledge that people take lying as an indicator of other misbehavior. As the thinking goes, "If you tell small lies, then why not big ones? And if you lie, maybe you also steal." I'm generally no fan of these so-called "slippery slope" arguments—the idea that one bad deed opens the door to bigger and worse ones. Most tax cheaters don't go on to build multibillion-dollar Ponzi schemes, and the student offering the old "The dog ate my homework" excuse won't automatically cheat on the SATs. But, at the very least, an inflated letter of recommendation may hurt the person I want to help and threatens to harm my reputation.

If that's not bad enough, what if the candidate somehow gets to see my letter and decides that I overstated her qualifications? Now the candidate knows I'm willing to bend the facts to give a leg up to someone I like. That is to say, the candidate likes me, and I like to be liked. I like friends, but this candidate has also learned that I will shade the truth for her. I've cast a shadow on my fairness. My integrity has taken a hit in her eyes.

So this exercise of asking, "What if?" is one part of what has been called a "test of publicity." A test of publicity considers what might happen when a lie is discovered. What if a judge finds out that a witness lied in court? What if a worker calls in sick and then is discovered on the tennis court? Asking and answering, "What if?" is enough to get most folks to tell the truth, or at least something pretty close to it.

## What If I Give My Applicant an Unfair Advantage?

So maybe I'm wrong and other references don't overstate the case for their applicants. Maybe my applicant isn't all that great. In yet another wrinkle in this gaming the process, some candidates are not fortunate enough to have a good reference in their corner; they lack access to an even mediocre reference. A better-suited candidate may be disqualified—through no fault of his own—in an atmosphere of privileged access to inflated recommendations.

Now, my candidate is the one with the advantage and, through my overstatement, gets better treatment than she deserves at someone else's expense. As much as I want her to advance, that's not right or just. Thanks to my overstatement, someone more deserving will be bumped by someone else who is less qualified.

## What Happens to the Admissions Process?

The integrity of the application process takes a hit when too many letter-writers go overboard. Imagine, again, an avalanche of little exaggerations going into a year's worth of applications and the responsibilities of those charged with reading the letters. That's some daunting task. Each overstatement makes that tough job even harder and puts a strain on the larger system. Now, you might wonder why my candidate or I should care about the integrity of the process. I'm just a rabbi at a temple, not a college admissions office or a scholarship evaluator, so I am not responsible for the system, I say to myself. But I also realize that we all have a share in the larger social processes. With enough lies—and, as we move ahead, there will be more than enough lying—our overall social fabric begins to fray.

## Try Truth Telling First

My takeaway from "Keep far from falsehood" on the one hand and examples of lying on the other? Follow the lessons of the Hebrew Bible, a book so honest that it faithfully describes what our people do, warts and all. The Hebrew Bible tells the truth, even when its favorite people don't.

Consider being truthful from the get-go. Begin with the truth, even if you are positive you are not going to tell it. After all, as they say, "honesty is the best policy." Professor Bok echoes this Jewish insight when she points out:

In any situations where a lie is a possible choice, one must first seek truthful alternatives. If lies and truthful statements appear to achieve the same result or appear to be as desirable to the person contemplating lying the lies should be ruled out. And only where a lie is a last resort can one even begin to consider whether or not it is morally justified.[1]

A lie should always begin with the truth. Starting with the facts leads the speaker to recognize the gap between the truth and the falsehood. It calls attention to the gaping moral difference between acting after thinking and acting without thinking at all. By actively deciding to lie, you'll be honest with yourself, and you'll be telling only one lie, not two. That is, you'll be lying to someone else, but you won't be lying to yourself as well.

So consider telling the truth about your friend's tie or your neighbor's cooking before deciding to lie. You'll be known for fearless candor, and you'll set an example of integrity that kids can follow. But be prepared to make a few enemies, too. Fortunately, Judaism approves of a lie intended to keep the peace, protect domestic harmony, or spare another person's feelings—even God will shade the truth to avoid causing embarrassment. Yet, putting honesty first helps prevent self-deception, and it sets up the opportunity for the self-reflection of Shabbat and the High Holy Days.

So far we have encountered some Jewish perspectives on the truth, falsehood, and much more. We have also seen how much Judaism values the goodness and potential of the individual, as when Abraham, Sarah, and their descendants make important contributions to Jewish life and continuity. We have witnessed perseverance when facing challenges, such as famine, a morally corrupt monarchy, and enslavement. The Hebrew Bible has also shown us that the future is good, with the forthcoming Exodus from Egypt, the revelation of the Hebrew Bible on Mount Sinai, and life in the Promised Land as examples of fulfillment of God's Covenant. All told, the Hebrew Bible is a wise partner for life.

Now we move from the little lies to the bigger ones.

Part III

# Big Lies

# Chapter 8

# Lying to Protect Oneself, Part 1

## The Family Narrative

Every family has a story, bringing author Bruce Feiler to consider the work of psychology professor Marshall Duke of Emory University and his colleagues.[1] Professor Duke studies the lessons kids learn from their own family stories by categorizing the children's narratives into three approaches.

First is the "ascending" story of a family on the rise, from bad to good. For instance, "We came to this country as poor immigrants. We worked, got educated, opened up a business, and now look at us, so successful today!" Next is the "descending" narrative of a family in decline, as life has gone from good to bad. For instance, "Once we were rich, and then we lost it all. Now look at us, nothing like we once were." Professor Duke finds that kids do best when a family takes a third approach he calls "oscillating," going up and down and ultimately up. For instance, "We had our highs and we had our lows. We lost a business and then we built a new one. We got sick and then returned to health." Telling the oscillating narrative, the honest reporting about good times and recovery from the bad, sets a positive example for coping with life's inevitable rejections, failures, and disappointments. This narrative teaches

67

kids that when life takes unwanted turns, it's possible to muster the wherewithal to carry on, fight, and make life good again. All in all, it's a realistic picture that nurtures a healthy emotional outlook. It tells kids to stay optimistic, refuse to give up, and persevere.

The oscillating narrative describes modern family life stories, just as it speaks to the family stories of the Hebrew Bible as well as the history of the Jewish people. The Hebrew Bible is a family's epic story, a multigenerational, oscillating narrative of smaller stories that all add up to one very big one, filled with plenty of highs and plenty of lows.

God puts Adam and Eve in charge of the Garden of Eden and gives them a few instructions: that's good. But when the first couple breaks the rules and get expelled from Eden, it is bad. Later, Adam and Eve have two sons, Cain and Abel, a wonderful turn of life until one brother kills the other in a fit of jealous rage. And on to Noah and the sad story of human corruption and the Great Flood immediately followed by the rebuilding of humanity, then on to the Covenant with Abraham and Sarah and beyond. My mentor, Rabbi Chaim Stern, of blessed memory, said the Hebrew Bible is filled with "an embarrassment of riches and a richness of embarrassments"—much to boast about and plenty to consider.

In and beyond the Hebrew Bible, the continuing panorama of Jewish history is an oscillating narrative, too. We lived and thrived in Israel for centuries, until the Babylonians destroyed Jerusalem and drove us from the land in 586 BCE. We returned to Jerusalem fifty years later to rebuild the city and our place of worship. We thrived until the Romans sacked our capital and Temple and again dispersed our people in 70 CE. Nevertheless, we continued to persevere and built the institution of the synagogue as the new center of Jewish life in our new homelands. Centuries later, for example, in Spain during the Golden Age, the brilliance of Maimonides and other great Jewish thinkers brought us to great intellectual heights, until our people suffered under the persecution of the Spanish Inquisition. From the Holocaust to the rebirth of Israel, Jewish history takes an oscillating narrative. Confronting and overcoming obstacles is an essential and historic Jewish spiritual responsibility.

Back to our own lives, where Professor Duke and his colleagues encourage families to tell the full story—good and bad, no matter how difficult it may be to tell it all or how hard it may be for kids to hear. Knowing the truth builds a child's sense of trust in the speaker, all the while modeling tenacity and fortitude. Honesty enhances a bundle of character attributes that make for success in life.

With this image of an oscillating narrative in mind, let's turn to the story of Abraham and Sarah and a lie of self-protection.

## My Wife Is My Sister

As we noted, famine hits Canaan, forcing Abraham and Sarah to abandon their homeland to sustain themselves in Egypt, where the Nile's water keeps the riverbanks fertile, even in times of drought. We read:

> As they approached Egypt and were about to enter, he said to his wife, Sarai, "Now I know you are a beautiful woman. When the Egyptians see you, they will say, 'This is his wife,' and they will kill me while letting you live. Please say that you are my sister so things go well for me thanks to you, and I will remain alive, thanks to you." (Genesis 12:11–13)

Drought strikes Canaan, and the first Hebrews strike a deal that keeps Abraham alive and free. Sarah is alive, too, but at the cost of having to go into a harem, at a very low point in the family history of the Jewish people.

This isn't the only time that our ancestors have to hit the road for food, nor is it the only time that one version or the other of the spouse-sibling ploy appears in Genesis. Just a few chapters later, Abraham and Sarah are living in Gerar in southern Canaan and face a similar situation with a similar outcome. Abimelech, king of Gerar, seizes Sarah for the harem, and Abraham presents himself as Sarah's brother (Genesis 20:1–18). This story line is echoed further on in Genesis when our ancestors Isaac and Rebecca find themselves suffering famine in Canaan (Genesis 26:1ff). Here, God tells Rebecca and Isaac to avoid Egypt and stay in Gerar under the protection of the Covenant. With some variations, the ruse "We are brother and sister, not husband and wife" repeatedly comes to the fore. The Hebrew Bible must love this spouse-sibling morphing, given the number of times we read it.

While I'm presenting the line as a lie, in another opinion—as we are seeing, there's almost always another opinion—Abraham and Sarah actually tell the truth when they say they are brother and sister. That is to say, the second rendition of the story informs us that they were half-siblings by the same father but a different mother (Genesis 20:12). Even so, at the very least, Abraham and Sarah are responsible for telling a half-truth, a half-lie of omission, for failing to disclose their marriage to the kings.

In the second version, God appears to King Abimelech in a dream with a warning that the king could expect to pay with his life for kidnapping Sarah, a married woman. In response to God, the king protests loudly for all to hear, saying he hadn't gone near Sarah, he had no idea she was married, and if he'd known she was married he would have left her alone to begin with. "Your guy, Abraham, lied to me, God. Why should I pay with my life for this patriarch's unscrupulous behavior?" This is an example of how a lie of omission, even if it's "just" a half-lie, can have serious consequences when taken as the whole truth. So, the husband-wife, brother-sister ruse is a lie, a half-truth at best. Now let's see what happens to Abraham and Sarah.

## Abraham Profits at Sarah's Expense

In the first version, Abraham asks Sarah to lie so that "things go well for me thanks to you, and I will remain alive, thanks to you"

(Genesis 12:13). Sure enough, Abraham makes out very well with this deal. The Hebrew Bible tells us:

> Pharaoh's ministers saw Sarah and praised her to Pharaoh, and they took the woman to Pharaoh's palace. Abraham benefited because of her. He got sheep, cattle, asses, male and female slaves, more asses and camels. (Genesis 12:15–16)

Abraham collects the goods while Sarah goes into lockdown, and the rabbis hit Abraham hard for greediness. This is Sarah, of all people, his wife. She selflessly leaves behind her birthplace, her home and loved ones, on the word of an invisible God, to found a new nation and a new faith in an unknown land. Is this how Abraham repays her loyalty and trust, abandoning her in captivity without standing up for her?

Rashi blasts Abraham by focusing on how the Hebrew Bible tells us that "Abraham said to himself, 'They will give me gifts'"[2] in anticipation of profiting at Sarah's expense. Nahmanides goes on to say that "Abraham the patriarch unintentionally committed a great sin" for lack of faith in God's Covenant that includes a pledge of personal security for our first Hebrews.[3] All in all, Abraham's lie is a cut-and-run lie of self-protection, intended to help no one but him. Now it may come as a surprise to see the rabbis criticize Abraham so severely, but the rabbis do. They don't mince words. When they are upset with someone, they say so. Let's look into this more deeply.

So it appears as though Abraham survives this scam and thrives, while Sarah pays the price. But before coming to a negative conclusion about Abraham, first let's recognize, as the Hebrew Bible says, "There was a famine in the land" (Genesis 12:10). In other words, the entire household faces the very real possibility of death by starvation in an era and in a place where no organized public assistance or international foreign aid program will rush to feed starving residents fleeing a drought-stricken region. It's easy to judge the Hebrew Bible people's decisions and behaviors harshly from the perspective of our own comfortable lives. To follow this line of thinking, we need to consider the morality of what they decide and the actions they take in their own context. They are under duress, in a life-or-death situation not of their own making, where no options are ideal. But we're not done yet.

While some rabbis appropriately challenge Abraham's motives and integrity, other rabbis rise to his defense. They excuse Abraham's behavior by pointing out that Abraham does not force Sarah into this conspiracy. He approaches her with the "magic word," "Please!" (Genesis 12:13). Abraham asks Sarah, he doesn't insist, and he leaves the final decision to her, so the rabbis say. But, on the other hand, how can she decline? Her husband's life is at stake. "Sorry, but no" may have meant his death. It is a no-win situation for Sarah.

Radak also takes Abraham's side, pointing out that Sarah's imprisonment is only temporary, that the king sends her away that very night; he never touches her.[4] To be sure, a shorter stay in sexual captivity—which is the honest way of speaking of a harem—is better than a longer one; I agree that living under temporarily intolerable circumstances is preferable to a permanent bad situation. But captivity is captivity. We need to do better than just say, "It didn't last long," because being held against one's will for just an hour is more than long enough.

In another attempt to defend Abraham, one midrash sees the brother-sister, harem-captivity tactic as a last resort, used only because another, better option fails (*Tanhuma, Lech Lecha* 5). Anticipating a problem when crossing into Egypt, Sarah hides in a locked box as the couple nears the border. When the customs officials question the contents, Abraham tries to convince them that the locked box holds barley. When the officials refuse to believe him, claiming it contains wheat that is taxed at a higher rate, Abraham offers to pay the higher tariff on wheat to avoid an inspection. When the officials say it is pepper, Abraham offers to pay that tax, too. The officials then claim that the box contains gold, and the midrash ends with them opening the box and finding something better—Sarah. Only after all this, say the rabbis in this midrash, do Abraham and Sarah claim to be siblings. The rabbis want us to know that Sarah and Abraham have no better option.

This midrash cleverly addresses three concerns. First, had the authorities believed Abraham, he would have paid the tariff, Sarah would have snuck in and avoided being forced into the harem, there would have been food, and that would have been that. The rabbis want to make sure we know that Abraham tries to protect Sarah's freedom and integrity and save his own skin, all at the same time. Unfortunately, the inside-the-box plan fails.

Second, anti-Semites have long used this brother-sister, husband-wife pretense, and other examples of lying in the Hebrew Bible, to indict all Jews as untrustworthy. Critics—from other faiths and people of no faith—have taken this incident to besmirch Jewish people as willing to profit off the heartache of others, even loved ones. So the rabbis address those negative concerns by claiming that Abraham offers to pay a larger than necessary customs tax out of pocket. Here is Abraham's nobility and courage: he puts money on the table and himself in jeopardy to preserve Sarah's honor. Third, and most critically, the rabbis go on to tell us that even though the locked-box tactic fails and Sarah goes into the harem, no one touches her when she is there, not at all.

In the first version, the Hebrew Bible itself tells us that "God inflicted plagues on Pharaoh" for taking Sarah captive (Genesis 12:17). Rashi adds, "He was smitten with the disease of *raaton*, which made intimacy difficult for him." In other words, a plague safeguarded Sarah's integrity. The second time, we don't have to go to the rabbis; again the Hebrew Bible tells us that King Abimelech of Gerar leaves Sarah alone (Genesis 20). The third time, the king of the Philistines realizes that Isaac and Rebecca are married when he catches them in the act (Genesis 26). The king orders everyone in the land to keep away from her, on pain of death. The point of all this, to the rabbis and the Hebrew Bible, is that the matriarchs are not forced into having sex.

As we have explored the lie of self-protection, we have seen how the rabbis approach the Hebrew Bible's people. Our rabbis can be very critical of our spiritual ancestors, as when they judge Abraham harshly for benefiting at Sarah's expense. Other times, the rabbis try to explain away negative appearances; for instance, when pointing out how Sarah remains untouched while in the harem. Whether accusing or defending, the rabbis put it all on the table. At the end of all the analysis, a lie of omission regarding marital status is still a lie, but in this case, that lie isn't a sin; it is rewarded.

So our oscillating narrative sees that a famine turns our ancestors into refugees, nearly forcing our people into extinction until a material and spiritual turnaround secures our continuity. We'll consider another dramatic oscillation in another lie of self-protection as brothers conceal their mischief in brazen misconduct, bringing this narrative to the bottom of the cycle.

## Chapter 9

# Lying to Protect Oneself, Part 2

It was a quiet week in Burlington, Wisconsin, between Christmas and New Year's in 1929, as the chiefs of police and fire sat around with their uniformed officers, passing time by seeing who could tell the biggest lie. The winner was the Burlington police chief, Frank Beller, who claimed never to have told a lie. Thus began the Burlington Liars Club, the club "founded on a lie." The Burlington tradition of lying for fame and folly continued each year after and carries on today.[1]

More recent winners included James Wilberg of Franklin, Wisconsin, with "There are three kinds of people in the world: those who are good at math, and those who are not"; Gareth Seehawer of Oconto Falls, Wisconsin, with "My grandson is the most persuasive liar I ever met. By the time he was two years old he could dirty his diaper and make his mother believe someone else had done it"; David Milz of Bristol, Wisconsin, with "I almost had a psychic girlfriend, but she left me before we met"; and Gary Gitzlaff of Kenosha, Wisconsin, with "I have an unwanted collection of chairs. It seems that every time I visit a doctor's office, the receptionist asks me to please take a chair, so I do."

The Burlington Liars Club honors the proverbial big fish story, told in earnest. As for this book, I can't blame you for thinking that we're convening the Canaan Liars Club, in that it seems to take a lie to get into that group, too.

## From Burlington to Canaan

The job description of a biblical patriarch requires skills in household administration and small business management, with a focus on nomadic and pastoral operations, human relations, family dynamics, and loyalty to God. To be sure, the patriarch Jacob has his hands full with his clan, the next generation having grown to twelve sons and one daughter in total. But instead of serving as the family's foundation of stability, as a patriarch should, Jacob inadvertently stokes jealousies. He makes sure that everyone knows that Rachel is his favorite wife and that the sons they had together—Joseph and Benjamin—are his favorites, too, with Joseph, in particular, enjoying junior VIP status.

Jacob fuels the sibling rivalries by encouraging Joseph, who "tattled on his brothers" (Genesis 37:2). Jacob is also known as Israel, and we read:

> Israel loved Joseph the most of all his sons, because he was the son of his old age. So, he made him a coat of many colors. (Genesis 37:3)

The coat exacts a hefty price when Joseph, the show-off, turns it into an in-your-face reminder of his higher status:

> When his brothers realized that their father loved him more than his brothers, they hated him and could not speak peacefully to him. (Genesis 37:4)

The Hebrew Bible's narrative takes a bad downturn when Joseph brags about dreams that put him at the center of the family. Never mind that this scenario comes true when the entire household relocates to Egypt.

There's no sin in dreaming, of course, not for Joseph or for anyone else. But Joseph's boasting and swagger pump up his brothers' rage. They catch Joseph alone in the countryside and hatch a vicious plan.

> "Now! Let's kill him and throw him into some pit and we'll say that a wild animal ate him. Then we'll see what will become of his dreams." (Genesis 37:20)

However:

> When Reuben heard this, he tried to save him from their hands. He said, "Do not kill him!" Reuben said to them, "Do not shed blood. Throw him into this pit here in the wilderness, but do not lay a hand on him." Reuben secretly planned to save Joseph from his brothers and bring him back to his father. (Genesis 37:21–22)

So the brothers abandon Joseph in a pit and then "they sat down to eat" (Genesis 37:25), callously indifferent to Joseph, who, for all they care, will die of thirst or starvation at the bottom of that hole in the ground.

## Lying with Indifference

Sissela Bok's book *Lying* came out just as the nation was absorbing the trauma of the Watergate break-in and President Richard Nixon's misrepresentations and resignation. She wrote of the Bob Woodward and Carl Bernstein account of the incident, *All the President's Men*:

> What is more troubling in the book than the lies themselves is the absence of any acknowledgment of a moral dilemma. No one seems to have stopped to think that there was a problem in using deceptive means. No one weighed the reasons

for and against doing so. There was no reported effort to search for honest alternatives, or to distinguish among different forms and degrees of deception, or to consider whether some circumstances warranted it more than others.[2]

That's quite a leap from the Hebrew Bible to Watergate, but the moral issue is the same: misbehavior without self-reflection. The Hebrew Bible affirms that acting without having "stopped to think that there was a problem" is one of the worst things a person can do. Now, let's get to the lie.

## "A Wild Animal Ate Him"

"Reuben returned to the pit, he saw Joseph was not there in the pit, so he tore his clothing" (Genesis 37:29) in distress, as a sign of mourning. Little do Reuben and Joseph's other brothers know that a passing caravan of slave traders, figuring there is money to make, pull Joseph up and out, bring him to Egypt, and sell him as a slave. Reuben

> returned to his brothers. He said, "The boy isn't there! I don't know where to go!" They took Joseph's coat, killed a young goat, and drenched the coat in the blood. They took the coat of many colors and brought it to their father and said, "We found this. Do you recognize it as your son's coat or not?" He recognized it and said, "My son's coat! A wild animal ate him, tearing Joseph to pieces." (Genesis 37:30–33).

A garment conceals the brothers' cruelty and misleads their father.
     The rabbis underscore that Jacob's playing favorites is a cause of heartache. They take this sorrowful incident as a warning to parents to treat their kids equally.

> Resh Lakish said in the name of Rabbi Elazar ben Azariah, who said: A person must not favor a child, because of

the coat of many colors that our patriarch Jacob made for Joseph. (*Genesis Rabbah* 84:8)

Of course, the rabbis know better than to blame all parents for all their kids' problems. As parents themselves, they well understand the realities and complications of family life. When they talk about parents, they are talking about their own situations. Nevertheless, they make it clear that Jacob makes big mistakes that compound a frightening and tragic chain of events.

As for our Hebrew Bible's oscillating narrative, Joseph rises from that empty pit, only to wind up back down, in jail for a crime he does not commit. He eventually rises to high office under Pharaoh when, out of admiration for Joseph's ability to anticipate events and manage them, Pharaoh appoints Joseph to oversee a national food storage program that will feed Egypt during a drought that Joseph foresees as so severe that even the waters of the Nile cannot irrigate the fields. Joseph brings his entire family to live in Egypt.

As we prepare to move ahead in this oscillating family narrative, we look back and see that one lie of self-protection enables the brothers to avoid responsibility for their misdeeds. Now, the brothers will spin another lie of self-protection intended to help them avoid having to pay for misconduct.

## "Your Father Commanded Us"

Though the entire family is living in Egypt when Jacob dies, they honor their promise to travel all the way back to Canaan to bury their father in an ancestral gravesite, the Cave of Machpelah. With Jacob dead and out of the picture, the brothers worry that Joseph will take advantage of his position and their powerlessness, and with the tables turned, exact revenge:

Joseph returned to Egypt: him, his brothers and all who went up with him to bury his father. After burying his father, Joseph's brothers, seeing their father was dead, said, "What if Joseph hates us? He will surely pay us back for the evil we did to him!" (Genesis 50:14–15)

Again, the Hebrew Bible never wastes a word; each word is there to teach, and the rabbis set out to tell us what the lessons of each and every one of those words happens to be.

The rabbis are troubled by what appears to be the Hebrew Bible's unnecessary comment "Joseph's brothers, seeing their father was dead." Of course the brothers knew their father was dead—we learned that in the previous chapter. Why would the Hebrew Bible tell us so a second time?

*Midrash Rabbah* says that the words "seeing their father was dead" mean that the brothers have noticed a change in Joseph.

They could see that he was dead by how Joseph behaved. They used to have dinner with Joseph and he welcomed them out of respect for his father. After Jacob's death, he didn't invite them. (Rashi to Genesis 50:15)

Were this a modern workplace, we'd be talking about a supervisor who suddenly acts differently toward you, stops inviting you to important meetings, or fails to include you in officewide emails. You know something is going on, you know it's not good, and you worry that something bad is about to happen.

The Midrash points out that Joseph stokes their anxiety by taking a little side trip on the way back from Jacob's burial:

Rabbi Isaac said: They worried that he had gone and looked into that pit. (*Genesis Rabbah* 100:8)

Joseph's stroll down memory lane to the scene of the crime shows that he is still brooding over the trauma, and the brothers are convinced that he will take advantage of the opportunity to get even.

After all, look at what the brothers did to him. They behaved very badly—at the rock-bottom of any oscillating family story. Joseph likely suffered years of emotional aftershocks following that ordeal of abandonment in an empty hole in the wilderness, being taken as a slave, jailed in Egypt for a crime he didn't commit, all in the absence of a family support network that any person deserves to have. So it is reasonable for the brothers to fear that Joseph will take revenge.

Looking to get out ahead of Joseph, and their own guilt and their fears,

> they told Joseph, "Your father commanded us, before his death, saying, 'This is what you say to Joseph: Please, I beg you, forgive your brothers and their sin. They hurt you. Now, please forgive the sins of the servants of your father's God.'" (Genesis 50:16–17)

Now wait just one minute. Jacob never says any such thing. Does he speak "off camera," outside the Hebrew Bible's reporting? No! The reality is that if the Hebrew Bible wants us to know such important words were spoken, it would have told us so. Besides, as far as the Hebrew Bible is concerned, Jacob never even learns the truth about the brothers throwing Joseph in the pit. As far as Jacob knows, his favorite son, Joseph, got kidnapped by slave traders when looking for his brothers in the wilderness—those things happened back then. Jacob has every reason to believe that his other sons were innocent of wrongdoing, so he has no need to tell Joseph to lay off.

Rashi and others claim that the brothers made it up. According to Rashi:

> *Your father commanded*: They changed the facts, saying something that was not true, for the sake of peace. Because Jacob had said no such thing, without Joseph in his sight.[3]

That is to say, the brothers acted less out of fear and more out of a noble motive, in hopes of fostering family harmony. But, as expected, other rabbis have other ideas, and they argue that Jacob really says all that. Sforno takes the words "before his death" to mean that "this happened then and we were not about to tell you about it then."[4] Jacob actually spoke to the brothers on the side.

Maybe Joseph is busy at work, managing the affairs of state, in Jacob's final moments. After all, he has a big job as Pharaoh's second-in-command, a combined position as minister of agriculture and social services, along with chief of staff, an all-consuming responsibility that takes him away from his family.

In any event, the Hebrew Bible explains that

> Joseph wept while they spoke. His brothers went and fell to the ground, saying, "Here we are, your slaves!" Joseph said to them, "Do not be afraid! Am I a stand-in for God? What you intended to hurt me, God intended for the good, to bring what we have today, to sustain a great nation. So now don't be afraid. I will provide for you and your children." He comforted them because he spoke to their hearts. (Genesis 50:17–21)

Joseph comes across as a very generously spirited guy who can put such awful memories behind him. But take a closer look. First, Joseph doesn't outright forgive the brothers—he doesn't say anything resembling "I forgive you." And why should he forgive them? For starters, they never apologize. Second, he places the whole business in God's hands. He leaves the entire decision and any punishment to God. So, it isn't even a faint-hearted kind of forgiveness, saying, "Let's just move on with life."

Joseph lets go but does not forgive or forget. The Midrash suggests that Joseph shows restraint out of self-interest, basically saying to himself:

What if I were to kill you? What would people say? If I kill you, they will say, "He saw a group of fine young men, and was proud of his relationship with them, saying, 'These are my brothers,' but afterward he killed them? Have you ever heard of a man killing his brothers?"[5]

Joseph realizes that the public doesn't know the backstory of the early days in Canaan. Doing the brothers in would make Joseph look bad and hurt his career. So Joseph lets the matter slide, more out of his work needs than out of any concern for his father's wishes, his brothers' well-being, or a desire to forgive them.

So, in the end, the brothers are lucky to get off with this bury-the-hatchet lie of self-protection. They are lucky that Joseph matures from the bragging, arrogant boy he once was.

The rabbis again excuse a lie about a father's words by underscoring the importance of social harmony, as we read:

Rabbi Shimon ben Gamliel taught: Great is peace because even our ancestors turned to a lie in order to make peace between Joseph and themselves. (*Genesis Rabbah* 100:8)

I'd say the same thing, too. I'd take a cold truce over a hot war, and that's what the Hebrew Bible does to advance familial harmony, even superficially. A guest would do well to temper a comment or compliment to a groom or a bride, just as God weighs words spoken to Abraham and when Sarah laughs, all as Joseph does here.

## Lying Comes Naturally

It is beginning to look as if lying is one of life's essentials, from Canaan to Burlington, on that short list of necessities, along with food, clothing, and shelter. Lying may come "naturally," and I am told that there is plenty of "lying" in nature. That is to say, animals instinctively put on pretenses to ward off predators and attract mates. Now I always think twice before making the leap from animal behavior, which tends to be instinct driven, to what we humans do, which relies more on decisions. But it is worth taking a look at human behavior in light of the rest of the natural world, which shows us that deception—though it may not be moral when people do it—happens often, unthinkingly, and without question in the world at large.

When it comes to fooling predators, nonpoisonous butterflies use the same wing patterns as poisonous species to avoid becoming another animal's next meal. Some birds turn on bio–false alarms against members of their own species to frighten off competitors for food. Among frogs, the bigger the male, the deeper the croak to scare off rivals and avoid a fight for some small patch of territory—and the mating opportunities that would follow—so smaller frogs figure out a way to croak more loudly.[6]

Lying seems to come as naturally to some of the Hebrew Bible's main characters as it does to birds and frogs. In the previous chapter, a married couple tries to pass themselves off as brother and sister to safeguard their personal interests and the well-being of the people. In this chapter, the brothers lie to avoid owning up to their bad behavior, as in a conspiracy that led a father to think an animal ate his son and a misrepresentation of a dying man's words.

We can all agree on the importance of honesty, full disclosure, and more, just as Professor Marshall and Bruce Feiler encouraged, for the days of the Hebrew Bible and our own times. Yet with all that has happened since the Hebrew Bible was first put to parchment, people still lie, and we lie often. According to journalist Megan Garber, writing in the *Atlantic Monthly*:

> Most of us lie, it turns out, with astounding regularity. According to a 2011 survey, people in the United States do so, on average, 1.65 times a day.... One in 10 text messages involves a lie of some kind. In a *Consumer Reports*

survey, one in four people admitted to falsifying information on Facebook. According to a study of online daters, a full 81 percent exaggerated their attributes on their dating profiles.[7]

Lying seems to be as important to life as breathing, if you accept these numbers. That is to say, while we breathe more often than we lie, we need to lie as much as we breathe, if you believe Pamela Meyer, author of *On How to Spot a Liar*, who also tells us:

> On a given day, studies show that you may be lied to anywhere from 10 to 200 times. Now granted many of those are white lies. But in another study it showed that strangers lied three times within the first 10 minutes of meeting each other. We lie more to strangers than we lie to co-workers. Extroverts lie more than introverts. Men lie eight times more about themselves than they do other people. Women lie more to protect other people.[8]

As it has been said by many, and phrased and rephrased in a variety of ways, "There are lies, damn lies, and then there are statistics," which makes statistics about lying the worst kind of lying there is. However, let's withhold judgment until after we consider the lie of self-advancement.

# Chapter 10

# Lying to Get Ahead

## Does He Need a Batting Coach or an Acting Coach?

Whenever a rabbi mentions baseball, you can expect smiles, jokes, and yawns, and it's probably something of a curveball for a book about the Hebrew Bible to turn to America's favorite pastime for an illustration. Nevertheless, I think you'll appreciate how the New York Yankees were barely clinging to first place in the American League East Division in mid-September 2010 during a game against the Tampa Bay Rays in Tampa. Tampa Bay was ahead 2–1 in the top of the seventh inning, with one out and no one on base. The Yankees' superstar shortstop Derek Jeter was in the batter's box until he was apparently hit by an 89 MPH pitch. Ouch! A pain-wincing Jeter grabbed his forearm, and the Yankees' manager and trainer bolted from the dugout to Jeter's side, worried that one of the most respected players in baseball was seriously injured. Jeter seemed to shake it off and took first base, just as the rules provide and the umpire directed.

I was watching the game that night as the slow-motion video replay made it 100 percent clear—and Jeter himself later admitted—that the ball didn't hit Jeter. It looked like the ball struck his forearm, but it actually nipped the round knob at the bottom of his bat. Jeter was acting, with the manager and trainer in supporting roles. Derek Jeter gave the umpire a runaround and advanced to first base on a lie.

The Rays' manager, a furious Joe Maddon, raced from the dugout to the umpire, demanding to know how anyone could miss the sound of a ball hitting a wood bat, a noise obviously audible in the visitors' dugout—as well as to everyone in the viewing audience, including me. As a Yankees announcer in the broadcast booth quipped, "You could hear that up here." In the days before Major League Baseball provided for video review of close plays, it was up to the manager to persuade the umpires. Maddon not only failed, but he was ejected from the game, and Jeter stayed on base.

The game went on, and the postgame analysis went on and on. "I really don't see what the big deal is," a puzzled Jeter said in the locker room after the game. "What am I supposed to do? Say, 'I'm sorry, sir, but it didn't hit me?' Next time somebody steals a base and a guy doesn't tag you, and the umpire calls you out, do you want the fielder to say, 'No, sir, I didn't tag him, let's just keep him here?'" As for the trainer's part in the foul play? Jeter smirked and said, "Geno acted more than I did, I guess." He continued, "I've been hit before and they said I wasn't hit. My job is to get on base, and fortunately for us it paid off at the time."

Jeter's fakery sparked a national media frenzy that included coverage in the *Wall Street Journal*, the *Chicago Sun-Times*, the *Boston Globe*, and more. The *New York Times* carried two pieces—a news article the day after the shenanigans and an ethical analysis and commentary in "The Week in Review."

One self-admitted Yankee hater argued that Jeter's antics were "perfectly consistent with the spirit of baseball." After all, and as many pointed out, there's no rule in baseball against lying. What's more, baseball lives on deception; there'd be no game without it. Pitchers trick batters into swinging into the air—will the ball drop, rise, or will it curve inward or away? Jeter and other fielders often fake a throw to fool a baserunner, only to take the hidden ball and snag the sucker between bases. Outfielders pretend to lose sight of a fly ball in the sun, throw both hands in the air as a call to other fielders to help, only to catch the ball and catch a runner off base in a double or even triple play. Like any sport, baseball thrives on sham. And I hear it now: "If a fielder can fake a throw and a runner can 'steal' a base, why can't a batter lie about being hit?"

What's more, people say that sham behavior in an umpired sport, like baseball, is very different from what happens off the field, outside the stadium, or in "real life." The umpire is ultimately responsible for deciding the truth during a baseball game, which gives players permission to say and do anything they want without any negative consequences; that's an incentive to be underhanded and outsource your moral compass. As former Yankees manager Joe Torre said, "It's not like running a red light. Stuff you can do out on the field, whether you can get away with it, it's not being immoral." So that's our question: Derek Jeter's behavior was technically legal, but was it ethical? Offered one sportswriter, as if dressed in mourning, "Today, Jeter has lost something, and baseball has lost something, and the rest of us have lost something, too."

As for me, I get plenty of exercise, but I'm not a professional athlete, and I don't know what I would recommend to someone in that situation. As I watched the close-up, slow-motion video replay on wide-screen TV from the comfort of my living room sofa, in Jeter's worst-case scenario—and I would add that I would hate to have anyone critique my work like that—a critic could argue that Jeter didn't have to throw the umpire an Oscar-worthy act. Jeter could have instead just dropped the bat and taken the base. There'd be no postgame backbiting, and you'd be reading about something else right now. But with apologies to legitimate actors, Jeter played it up, and his manager and trainer joined the act, leaving us to call in an ethicist—instead of an ambulance—over a lie that advanced a player to first base.

As for other comments about this late-summer snow job? Rays manager Joe Maddon said after the game, "There are several thespians throughout baseball. I thought Derek did a great job, and I applaud it, because I wish our guys would do that same thing." Sanguine and envious. Yankees manager Joe Girardi said, "I think if it wasn't Derek Jeter, and it wasn't that series, I don't think people would talk about it. This happens all the time ... I think because of who it is it's become a big deal." And it sure became a "big deal."

I'm not sure what to say about ethics in an umpired sport like baseball, where the umpires—the men in black—are the on-base cops. Yet, there's something sleazy in the lie to advance oneself, whether in baseball, another sport, or elsewhere. You probably got the typo-filled emails allegedly coming from a foreign prince offering to share a multimillion-dollar inheritance in exchange for your advance of several hundred dollars. And you probably got the email, purportedly from the friend you saw for lunch yesterday, with the heartbreaking story of being trapped at the Manila airport, broke, begging you to wire money to help pay for a return flight. The lie spun to advance oneself is one of the worst kinds of lies a person can tell, and we will see that kind of lie in the sibling rivalry between Esau and Jacob.

## Inheritance and Sibling Rivalry

Inheritance was pretty much a zero-sum game in biblical days, with the oldest son getting most of it, if not all. So you can imagine what family dinners must have been like back then, especially in a home with twin brothers, where just a few seconds at birth made all the difference. Now we turn to Esau and Jacob, whose early life story is an oscillating narrative threatening to wobble off the family story charts.

This brotherly feud begins even before birth, as the Hebrew Bible describes Rebecca's report of an unusual amount of kicking in utero. The Midrash explains that each boy is trying to escape from the womb to pursue something emblematic of his character and values. Rebecca would be out and about on errands and

> when she passed the doors of the school of Shem and Ever,
> Jacob struggled and tried to get out; the doors of idolatry,
> Esau tried to get out.[1]

If it's not enough of a fantasy to say that Esau wants to worship idols while Jacob wants to study the Hebrew Bible during their mother's pregnancy, what on earth is this "Shem and Ever" school of Torah study, hundreds of years before the Hebrew Bible comes to be?

The Shem and Ever school exists in the mind of the rabbis. The rabbis love the Hebrew Bible; its teachings are so critical to their lives that they can't imagine a world without *mitzvot* regulating diet, Shabbat, and the rest of Jewish practice. So, the rabbis dream about a Jewish academy back then in the wilderness, where a nomad kid learns it all.

I know that this kind of Jewish make-believe raises sighs of exasperation among the more rational-minded among us. Let's keep in mind that this school of Shem and Ever has nothing to do with historical fact or fiction. The real issue has to do with each of us being open to Jewish fantasy. Simply put, being good at Torah study means having a good sense of humor. As much as the rabbis revere the Hebrew Bible, they also enjoy talking about it, discussing and challenging each other. The rabbis keep words of the psalmist in mind, the suggestion to "serve God with joy" (Psalm 100:2). So I take this daydream of Hebrew Bible study before there is a Hebrew Bible as an example of the rabbis having a good time talking about the Jewish teachings that they love so deeply, that this school of Shem and Ever is the product of hyperbole, concocted to drive home a point about the importance of Torah study and taking enjoyment in that endeavor. There's no need for a bagel and coffee as an incentive to get anyone to come to Torah study in the days of the rabbis—having a good time is motivation enough. Of course, some are still convinced that "fun" and "Hebrew Bible" don't belong in the same sentence, and if you feel that way, you probably would not have read this far into this book. Talking about Shem and Ever is an example of the imaginative ways the Hebrew Bible speaks to the lives and dreams of our rabbis, just as it speaks to how we learn Torah together.

Back to our text. Rebecca is so tormented by the struggle of the boys within her that she seeks out an opinion from God who replies:

> Two nations are in your womb,
> Two nations will come from within you.
> One will be stronger than the other,
> The older shall serve the younger.
>     (Genesis 25:23)

Here we have one more "Just So" story. The prophecy and the birth explain why the people of Israel don't get along with the nation of Edom. "Just so," each boy represents a different people, very different from the start.

Just so, the descendants of red-haired, hotheaded Esau grow into the nation of Edom, looking and acting a lot like their forebear, Esau. Meanwhile, the people of Israel, Jacob's descendants, have the same smooth skin and deliberative personality that the Hebrew Bible attributes to Jacob. The boys are physical twins but constitutional opposites. One is an impulsive, athletic outdoorsman, while the other is a calculating, bookish thinker. And with one wanting to go to school, the other wanting to go out and play with idols, the Hebrew Bible sets the stage for a rivalry that continues for many, many years, long after the brothers have died. The Hebrew Bible tells the story of a birth rivalry to pinpoint the beginning of a difference and a rivalry between nations. Different nations inherit the different personalities of their founders, differences apparent at birth, even before, "just so."

Rebecca goes into labor, Esau is born first, and Jacob, grasping Esau's heel, emerges immediately afterward. That's how Jacob gets his name: *Ekev* is Hebrew for "heel," corresponding to *Ya'akov*.

The Hebrew Bible uses names to foreshadow future events; the teaser of a birth struggle leaving a brother to lose by a heel promises that another, bigger fight will be coming. From the very first breath, the younger brother keeps at the heel of the older brother; the differences are hardwired from the start. The story of the birth of the twins builds suspense for a high-stakes competition to follow: the fight over inheriting the family mantle and leadership of the nation.

I know that we haven't gotten to the lie yet. We are still setting the backdrop with selections that showcase the Hebrew Bible's gifts of insight of a family therapist, an international political analyst, and a great entertainer. And we are getting closer to that lie.

An opportunistic Jacob skillfully finagles a birthright from a famished and impulsive older brother, Esau. But the birthright isn't worth much to Jacob without their father's end-of-life blessing. It only gets him to first base, far from home and winning the game or the World Series. Now Jacob sets off to gain that title, too.

## "I Am Esau, Your Firstborn"

Isaac, realizing his death is approaching, asks his firstborn, Esau, to cook up the traditional dinner, as was the custom at the time, part of the Hebrew Bible's ritual of the day when getting a father's final blessing. While Esau is Isaac's favorite, Jacob is Rebecca's. Rebecca overhears Isaac's conversation with Esau and gives her beloved Jacob a "heads-up":

> "Go to the flock. Bring me two tender kids. I will make them into tasty dishes that your father likes. You bring them to your father, and we will eat so that he blesses you before he dies." (Genesis 27:9–10)

Any meat meal was a big deal in the days of the Hebrew Bible, long before refrigeration and mass-produced, prepackaged, cut-up chicken or frozen hamburgers, ready to throw right on the grill. You raised the meat or hunted it yourself in Bible times. You killed it, cleaned it and cooked it, and you ate it on the spot. You didn't do all that kitchen work every day, making any meat meal a very special occasion, even without the family inheritance and national destiny in the balance. Rebecca offers to do all the cooking, but Jacob balks anyway, afraid of getting caught as an imposter. He says,

> "My brother is a hairy man and I am smooth-skinned. If my father touches me, he will recognize me as an imposter and I will bring on myself a curse, not a blessing." But his mother said to him, "Your curse will be on me, my son. Just listen to me and get these things for me." (Genesis 27:11–13)

Rebecca offers to shoulder the responsibility for hatching and orchestrating the ruse, so it can be argued that Jacob doesn't do anything wrong here. He merely honors his mother's instructions, just as the fifth of the Hebrew Bible's Ten Commandments later demands of a child with respect to a parent. (Jacob no doubt learns about this mitzvah in the school of Shem and Ever.) But as surely as the Ten Commandments insist that a child behave with respect to *both* parents, that a person honors both father *and* mother, Jacob is caught in the middle, in a double effect, between obeying his mom and respecting his dad, and in this zero-sum, winner-take-all family scenario, Jacob decides to honor Mom.

Yet midrash also exonerates Jacob by blaming Rebecca. When Jacob "went to get them and bring them to his mother" (Genesis 27:14), "he acted under duress, bowed over and weeping" (*Genesis Rabbah* 65:15), as if to say he really doesn't want to go ahead with it, poor guy.

Another midrash exonerates both Rebecca and Jacob by holding God responsible. Rebecca is just faithfully fulfilling God's prediction when she is pregnant. As mentioned, God says:

Two nations are in your womb,
Two nations will come from within you.
One will be stronger than the other,
The older shall serve the younger.
(Genesis 25:23)

So this midrash sees the responsibility as God's, as if a God of truth is encouraging this misrepresentation. But let's go deeper.

It must have looked like Purim to an outsider, long before the holiday came to be, to see Jacob scurrying from tent to tent with a bowl of stew in his hands while costumed in furry goatskins to feel hairier when touched by his blind father. Despite all of Jacob's efforts, Isaac is nevertheless suspicious from the start.

Jacob went to his father, saying, "My father!" and he said, "Here I am. Which one of my sons are you?" Jacob replied to his father, "I am Esau, your firstborn." (Genesis 27:18–19)

That's Jacob's lie: "I am Esau, your firstborn." But before deciding that Jacob lies or that his lie is also a sin, let's withhold judgment until all the rabbis weigh in.

Rashi is convinced that Jacob is telling the truth to his father, that Jacob isn't lying at all. How? Rashi carefully studies the Hebrew Bible's original words, "I am Esau, your firstborn," and takes the Hebrew to mean, "It's me. Esau is your firstborn,"[2] and that is a legitimate reading of the text, too. In other words, Rashi wants us to think that Jacob is being honest, owning up to who he is, and puts the responsibility for the blessing on Isaac.

I imagine that Rashi was deeply embarrassed by Jacob's egregious lie. After all, Rashi and his colleagues faced up to Hebrew Bible critics who misappropriated this story and others to attack Jewish belief, practice, and people. The hostile environment backed our rabbis into a corner, and they responded with innovative explanations to harmonize the moral fabric of Judaism with the questionable behavior of our patriarchs. And you know what? Either translation is consistent with the Hebrew Bible text. Now, to delve deeper, is Rashi correct? Is Isaac in on this deal?

## Is Isaac a Coconspirator?

Isaac appears to fit the classic and unfortunate negative comic stereotype of the bumbling, confused elder, a popular portrayal of older folks until people recognized the need to stop making fun of people's age and their physical limitations. What's more, upon closer scrutiny, Isaac doesn't fit that tired stereotype, either. Isaac is blind, but the Hebrew Bible wants us to know that he has the rest of his faculties—he can hear, smell, touch, and taste.

Isaac can hear and recognize the difference between Esau's voice and Jacob's voice. We know he smells the difference between the boys, saying that he loves the way Esau's nature smell reminds him of the fields. Isaac feels the difference between animal skin and human skin. After all, even the hairiest human skin doesn't feel like a goat's—how hairy can a guy get? Isaac must know something fishy is going on when he tastes the dinner. There's a big difference between the taste of domesticated goat meat and the taste of wild venison—I've eaten both and know the difference, too. Isaac knows he is blessing Jacob instead of Esau; he buys into the stunt, just as Rashi suggests. But why doesn't he just bless Jacob outright? What does he gain by pretending?

Good question. Isaac goes along with the plot to buy himself cover when facing Esau. Isaac plays into this arrangement because he doesn't want to confront Esau with the truth—that Isaac and Rebecca believe that Jacob is the better choice as family leader. By placing the blame on Jacob, Isaac has it both ways. He appoints Jacob head of the household and preserves his relationship with Esau.

When Esau learns that Jacob has gotten in ahead of him, he asks to be blessed as well. Isaac says there is only one firstborn blessing, it went to Jacob, and that is that. It would be impossible to bless Esau, too, because "your brother came with deceit and took your blessing" (Genesis 27:35).[3] Jacob, the heel, sneaks in ahead of Esau, by a heel, in a script worthy of any successful TV crime or comedy show. But Jacob's double-dealing comes at the hefty price of driving a wedge between the brothers and creating a rift in the family. The lie of self-advancement gets Jacob to first base, but he is not safe at home, not by any means. Now, we have to address that other issue before moving ahead with Jacob's lies of self-advancement.

## Back to Baseball

A home run scored Jeter and put the Yankees ahead. When Jeter stepped up for his next at-bat, his earlier gaming of the game earned the taunting chants of "Jeter, cheater!" The Yankees lost that night, allowing Tampa Bay to take the division lead by a half-game and to go on to finish the season in first place, with the Yankees right behind them—by a "heel"—in second, with a "wild card" long-shot chance to advance through the playoffs. After the regular season ended, the Yankees lost their one playoff game, ending their flirtation with the divisional and league titles and the World Series.

Jeter's deception came to naught, whereas Jacob's deception paid off. But let's see what happens when Jacob wrestles with his uncle Laban. Jacob, who pretends to be his brother, is about to meet up with the woman who pretends to be her sister.

## He Saw It Was Leah!

Jacob reacts to Esau's threat by fleeing from home to Padan Aram, to live with his uncle Laban. Jacob approaches Laban's neighborhood, first stopping at the local watering hole. There he chances to meet his cousin Rachel, and it is love at first sight. The Hebrew Bible goes on to tell us that "when Laban got word about his nephew Jacob, he ran to greet him. He hugged him, kissed him, and brought him to his home" (Genesis 29:13). But don't take Laban's embrace at face value. Laban has ulterior motives.

You'd expect a house gift from a houseguest, so Laban is surprised when Jacob arrives empty-handed. Say what you want about Laban, but give him credit for what he has going for him, which includes a good memory for things he considers important.

Laban recalls that Abraham's servant arrived years earlier on a similar mission to find a wife for his boss's son, that is, Jacob's dad, Isaac. The servant picked Rebecca as Isaac's match and made a generous payment of a caravan full of goods in exchange for her. Laban remembers that large lump sum and knows that Jacob is single. Laban thinks of his two daughters, Rachel and Leah, and suspects that there would be money for him in welcoming this visitor. As the Midrash points out, Laban

> figured that Eliezer, the servant, was a lowly householder, but it is written of him, "The servant took ten camels" [Genesis 24:10]. This one, Jacob, the beloved of his home, how much the more so! (*Genesis Rabbah* 70:13)

Jacob carries no baggage, leaving Laban to wonder, "Where are the goods?" Laban knows not to trust appearances, so when Laban

> did not even see Jacob's wallet, "he embraced him" [Genesis 29:13] thinking he may be hiding money in his belt. Finding nothing, "he kissed him" [ibid.], thinking he may be hiding precious stones in his mouth. Said Jacob, "You think I am carrying a fortune? I am carrying nothing but words," and so, "He told Laban everything" [ibid.]. (*Genesis Rabbah* 70:13)

And Laban responds with "You surely are my bone and my flesh!" (Genesis 29:14), as if to say, "You are just as much a crook as me!" Those words of welcome turn out to be true, and as we shall see, Laban is no less the rascal than Jacob.

Jacob asks to marry Rachel. Penniless, Jacob agrees to Laban's proposition, that seven years of Jacob's labor would be an appropriate payment for this marriage. But when the seven years pass and it comes to the wedding night, Laban tricks Jacob. Instead of bringing Jacob his chosen, Rachel, Laban brings Leah to Jacob, who cannot tell the difference at night.

> In the morning he saw she was Leah. He said to Laban, "What did you do to me? Didn't I work for you for Rachel! Why did you deceive me?" (Genesis 29:25)

Jacob protests, and Laban responds, "It must not be done so in our country, to give the younger before the firstborn" (Genesis 29:26). Unfortunately, Laban does not tell this to Jacob beforehand, and this failure of disclosure leads Jacob to act differently than he would have had he known the truth. Jacob gets away with usurping his older brother's position, but Laban will not let Rachel do the same to Leah.

Laban is guilty of deceiving Jacob and the Midrash wants us to know that Leah is equally guilty of pulling the wool over Jacob's eyes. See what happens when Leah arrives to be with Jacob in the dark:

> The entire night, he called her Rachel and she responded. In the morning, "She was Leah!" [Genesis 29:25]. He said to her, "You are a deceiver and the daughter of a deceiver! Didn't I call you Rachel during the night? And didn't you respond to me?" She said to him, "Is there a teacher without pupils? Didn't your father call you 'Esau' and you answered him?" (*Genesis Rabbah* 70:13)

What goes around, comes around, with the goat meat cooked up as pseudo-venison and ersatz hairy arms of the previous chapter now bringing Jacob repayment in kind for his deceptive behavior. Jacob's lie is a sin and it costs him; this lie is not rewarded. The

Hebrew Bible doesn't explicitly condemn Jacob's behavior. It simply tells the story and leaves judgment to us.

## Jacob Is Responsible

As we close consideration of Jacob's character, we can choose to accept Rashi's interpretation of the Hebrew Bible text and come away from this story thinking that Jacob is an honest guy by being up front with his father, Isaac, and the responsibility for deception falls on Jacob's dad. But first, recognize that Jacob collects all the benefits of getting in ahead of his brother, including the blessing, the birthright, and the family mantle. What's more, after Jacob later wrestles that name change, Israel, out of an angel that dark night by the Jabbok River, the entire nation takes on that name, Israel, from then to today. Jacob gets all the rewards. While many have tried to defend Jacob's behavior, no one can say that Jacob behaved nobly, even though he appears to be the better choice to become the leader. Yet we have more to discuss when it comes to lies to advance oneself.

While Jacob gets all the advantages, the Hebrew Bible notes that his uncle Laban evens the score. Jacob's mistreatment at Laban's hand stands as a warning: selfish deeds eventually receive comeuppance later in life.

Jacob's life isn't easy. His brother threatens to kill him and forces him to flee from home for his life. He is hoodwinked by Laban and Leah, loses his beloved wife, Rachel, prematurely, and mistakenly believes his favored son, Joseph, is dead. No wonder Jacob looks back from his old age and reflects, "Few and hard have been the years of my life" (Genesis 47:9). Jacob never regains his spiritual balance, even with all that he and his family achieve.

## Pretending to Be Someone You're Not

Jacob's life story teaches that pretending to be someone else has its advantages—until it doesn't. Yet all these centuries later, people continue to misrepresent themselves to advance themselves, to their eventual personal detriment. As much as they move ahead, in the end they wind up the worse for it.

Everybody knew that Oregon congressman Wes Cooley had served with the Army's Special Forces in Korea—until people learned he was lying. Republican Party officials pressured him to drop a 1996 reelection bid, and he was convicted of making a false claim in an official document.

Everyone knew that federal judge James Ware of California had a brother murdered in a racist shooting in Alabama. He told this story for years until acknowledging that the tragedy happened to a different Birmingham family with the same name. He then asked President Bill Clinton to withdraw his nomination for a higher judicial post.

Ferdinand Waldo DeMara Jr., the inspiration for the 1960 movie *The Great Impostor*, "borrowed" other people's names and credentials to pursue a varied and colorful series of careers. He worked as an assistant warden at a Texas prison, a dean of philosophy at a Pennsylvania college, and a teacher in Maine. During the Korean War, he posed for several months as a surgeon on a Canadian destroyer, suturing wounds and performing minor operations.[4]

A faked resume opens doors, yet it is nothing more than a lie to advance oneself. Like anyone else who lies, a person submitting a bogus resume runs the risk of discovery, making that test of publicity all the more critical as a predictor of what may happen if the lie is uncovered.

In the next chapter, we'll examine the vindictive lie that brings no personal benefit or protection, other than the warped pleasure of seeing someone else suffer.

# Chapter 11

# Lying to Hurt Others

## Schadenfreude

If you've ever laughed when the *schlemiel* spills the soup on the *schlimazel* (the classic Yiddish scenario when a clumsy waiter serves an unlucky customer), you've experienced the meaning of the German word "schadenfreude," taking pleasure in someone else's misfortune.

Schadenfreude makes TV comedy funny and TV crime criminal. There's schadenfreude when a crook or murderer gets what he deserves and justice prevails. There's schadenfreude in the gleeful delight of political commentators when skewering those with opposing opinions. And, yes, there is schadenfreude when the nuns help the Von Trapp family of *The Sound of Music* get the better of the Nazis.

There's schadenfreude in the Hebrew Bible, too. Isn't it great that the stubborn Pharaoh of Egypt gets his due during the ten plagues? What could possibly be wrong in enjoying a little schadenfreude there? But let's see how schadenfreude works hand in hand with lying. There's particular vindication in a lie told to get even, but unfortunately for the Torah's Joseph, he becomes the victim.

# He Tried to Rape Me

Joseph rises from that empty pit to a responsible position as an Egyptian middle manager, chief servant to Potiphar. But no sooner does Joseph seem secure than his life takes another sudden downturn.

> One special day, he came into the house to do his work. None of the household were there in the house. She stripped his garment and said, "Lie with me." He left his garment in her hand and fled outside. When she saw he had left his garment in her hand and fled outside, she called out to her servants and said, "See! He, my husband, brought us a Hebrew man to play around with us. He came to me to lie with me, and I cried out in a loud voice. When he heard me raise my voice and cry out, he left his garment with me and fled outside." She kept his garment with her until her husband came home. She told him all this, saying, "The Hebrew slave approached me, the one you brought us, to play around with me. When I raised my voice, and cried out, he left his garment with me and fled outside." When his master heard his wife's words, that is to say, "Your slave did these things to me!" he was furious. (Genesis 39:11–19)

You have to feel sorry for Joseph, who winds up in jail, punished for a crime he did not commit.

What's more, Joseph holds his ground, nobly refusing Potiphar's wife. He should have been rewarded for his self-discipline instead of being sent to jail to suffer. So the rabbis take Potiphar's wife to task for her lie. Rashi views the Torah's words, "One special day," to mean exactly when Potiphar's wife decides to strike.

> It was on a day of celebration, a day of their sacred feast when everyone went to the temple of their idols. She said, "I

won't find a better day than this to be with Joseph." So she told her attendants, "I am sick and cannot go to the temple."[1]

She lies to her attendants, she lies about Joseph, and she lies to her husband about Joseph. And she is very calculating all through her lying. Just as she waits for the right moment to trap Joseph, she also waits again for the right time to spring this lie on her husband:

> *And it came to pass when his master heard*: Rabbi Abahu said: When they were in bed. (*Genesis Rabbah* 87:9)

The reality is that Joseph gets off lucky, even with all that heartache. As we see of Potiphar:

> *He was enraged*: But didn't kill him, because he knew to be suspicious of the claim.[2]

Ibn Ezra leads us to think that Potiphar has already been down this road with his wife, that she's an Egyptian take on the legendary "boy who cried wolf" with a history of lying.

So Potiphar's wife takes vindication in schadenfreude and goes on with her life, while Joseph goes directly to jail. The Hebrew Bible shows its dislike for Potiphar's wife by denying her the honor of mentioning her name, leaving her to head off into history in anonymity, whereas Joseph rises from that prison to become Egypt's second-in-command.

## Limits to Schadenfreude

The innocent Joseph suffers to the satisfaction of his detractor. On the other hand, there's nothing wrong with a little schadenfreude when bad things happen to bad people and evildoers get what they deserve. But, even then, the rabbis want us to temper any display of satisfaction. When your enemy falters and suffers, don't brag or gloat.

Later on, in Exodus, Pharaoh has a change of heart when the ten plagues end and the people of Israel leave Egypt for freedom. Pharaoh wants us back as slaves and leads his soldiers on horses and chariots in hot pursuit of the people of Israel into the Sea of Reeds. By some miracle we don't drown: The waters part, the seabed dries out, and we walk across to the safety of the opposite shore. As for our attackers:

> The waters returned and covered the chariots and the chariot drivers, the entire army of Pharaoh that followed them into the sea. Not one survived. But the people of Israel walked on the dry seabed, the waters as a wall for them on their right and on their left. (Exodus 14:28–29)

The angels break out in song as the Egyptian army drowns, until, as Rabbi Shmuel ben Nahman says, God silences them by saying, "My creatures are dying and you are singing praises?" (Talmud, *Sanhedrin* 39b). That is to say, it's OK to feel vindicated. Just don't launch into a song and dance.

Judaism doesn't want us too pumped up when those who try to harm us stumble. Yet it would be impossible to ban schadenfreude entirely, any more than any other emotion, by telling people, "Don't feel that way!" Being human means experiencing a broad range of emotions, including firsthand experience with what schadenfreude is all about.

So there are lies told to harm others, just as there are lies told to protect others, as we will see when we turn to the noble lie.

# Chapter 12

# The Noble Truth and the Noble Lie

My mentor, Rabbi Chaim Stern, of blessed memory, loved this example of an ethical dilemma: "You co-own a small business, and you are at the cash register. A customer pays for a purchase with a $20 bill, and as you reach for change, you discover that you are holding two $20 bills stuck together, unbeknownst to the customer. So here's the ethical dilemma: do you tell your business partner?"

Chaim was joking, of course. He knew you'd return the extra cash. It's moral and noble, and it makes good business sense. Where else can you buy so much goodwill for $20 that's not even yours to begin with? It's a steal. But, in all seriousness, let's take on the perspective that sometimes truth telling is noble and sometimes it's noble to lie, as we consider a variety of related situations.

## Scienter

Sometimes you just have to tell the truth.

It varies from situation to situation and state to state, but there are occasions when the law expects a person to tell it all. "Scienter" is the legal term for knowing about something significantly wrong, or "guilty knowledge." Let's say your neighbor puts a car on the market. The car has a serious brake problem, but the seller doesn't tell anyone about this potentially life-threatening issue when the car is listed for sale. Scienter is guilty knowledge of a probable significant matter that the seller is under a legal obligation to disclose, even to the point of putting herself in a compromising position. This isn't noble truth; it's truth telling in self-protection—you'd pay for it under the law if you tried to hide it.

## When a Lie Is Expected

Taking a lighter situation as an illustration, you've accepted an invitation to a surprise birthday party for one of your best friends, and you promised to keep it all a secret. You run into the birthday person, who asks, "Be honest. What's up Saturday?" and you respond by lying, "Nothing I know about," because that's what you promised— you promised to lie. Now let's keep in mind that this is one of your best friends. You went out and bought a gift and kept it all a secret, through text messages, calls, and now when being questioned in person. Yet, the morning after the party, you don't get, "How could you betray me?" Instead, you hear, "How did you manage to keep it a secret?" You honored your word to one person by lying to another, and it all turned out just fine.

Turning from a surprise party to another example, that of haggling, some people are born to bargain. For others, like me, it's an acquired skill that I never acquired. I avoid flea markets and garage sales, but when I'm in Israel, I can't resist the back-and-forth of bargaining in the market they call the *shuk*. I've gotten caught up in the quibbling over the quality of the merchandise, how much it's really worth, what I'm willing to spend, and how much the seller is willing to take. The negotiations typically reach a stalemate, and then the cat-and-mouse sequence comes into play.

There's not much nobility when I turn and start to leave the shop, only to freeze in place when I hear, "Hey! Wait! I'll let you have it for three shekels less"—not the "final price" I demanded, but good enough. Or, just as often, the shopkeeper holds firm, and I walk out the door, only to think about it and return a few minutes later, willing to give him what he is asking for, but it just got five shekels higher—take it or leave it. The point is that when it comes to haggling, a good lie is expected; other times, too. You're writing a novel, a work of fiction, and your reader expects you to make it all up. Or, lying is part of the fun when you're an actor onstage, pretending to be someone else. Again, pretending is expected. No nobility here on any level—business is business.

Take that old and popular TV game show *To Tell the Truth*. Despite the name, some of those onstage were expected to lie. *To Tell the Truth* featured a panel of three contestants—a real guest with an unusual occupation who promised "to tell the truth" and two imposters. So, imagine a panel including a real-life astronaut-in-training accompanied by a librarian and a funeral director as imposters. Or think of a professional wrestler alongside two imposters—a clergy member and an accountant. Then, there was a second panel composed of four celebrities. This panel was charged with correctly sorting out the real contestant from the imposters.

The show's host read a description of the real guest and then invited the celebrities, one by one, to question all the guests with an eye toward sorting out fact from fabrication. At the end of the round of questioning, the host asked the celebrity panelists to openly vote on who they thought was legit, and when the votes were in, the host asked, "Will the real 'so-and-so' please stand up?" The real contestant would rise, the imposters would give their true names and describe what they really did in life. Applause, commercial break, and then on to the next panel of contestants. No nobility here—it's all entertainment.

So, the contestant on *To Tell the Truth* was responsible for telling the truth; the real guest had to own up. But, you'd better lie if you were one of the show's imposters or if you're trying to keep a surprise party a surprise or you're bargaining at the market. Let's now go back to the Hebrew Bible and times, as in our opening examples, when a person is obligated to tell the truth because there's little room to lie, if any.

## "Shall I hide from Abraham?"

The Hebrew Bible takes the story of Sodom and Gomorrah as an illustration of the responsibility to behave truthfully. God believes that destruction of the cities is in order and could have just gone ahead and done it, but feels obliged to tell Abraham first. God asks rhetorically, "Shall I hide from Abraham what I am about to do?" (Genesis 18:17). According to Rashi, God says, "It is not proper for me to do this thing in Sodom without him knowing. I gave him this land."[1] The rabbis take God's self-reflection as a lesson on the importance of respecting the title of ownership and honoring the integrity of one's word. We are to follow God's noble example of truthfulness in situations like these and tell the truth, even when truth telling comes at a very high cost, as we will see in Joseph's case.

## Joseph Brings Back Bad Reports to Their Father

Young Joseph had a way of incurring his brothers' wrath. Joseph primes their father with a continual flow of gossip about his sibs, as the Hebrew Bible says, "Joseph brought bad reports back to their father" (Genesis 37:2), to which Rashi adds that he went out of his way to cast them in a bad light to his advantage. In other words, Joseph tells the truth, but his talebearing is as noble as it is self-serving, and all this honesty boomerangs to Joseph's detriment. As we have also seen, Jacob, Joseph's father, further undermines family peace by rewarding the talebearing by giving Joseph that coat of many colors.

Things then reach a crisis point when Jacob instructs Joseph to go out and gather more tales:

> "Please go look in on the well-being of your brothers and the well-being of the flock and bring me back word." (Genesis 37:14)

While the Hebrew Bible allows a reader to think of Joseph as nothing more than a tattler, the rabbis clarify that. Joseph tells on his brothers only because they behave very badly. According to the Midrash, Joseph reports to Jacob as follows:

> Rabbi Meir said: "Your children are suspected of eating limbs torn from living animals." Rabbi Yehudah said: "They bully the sons of the concubines and call them slaves." Rabbi Shimon said: "They sexually harass the local girls." (*Genesis Rabbah* 84:7)

The brothers act so heinously, according to Rabbis Meir, Yehudah, and Shimon, that Joseph has no other option than to do what he does, that is, reporting the entire unvarnished truth to their father. And, I can imagine that the brothers really do all that, given how awfully they later behave toward Joseph. We see Joseph's brothers' capacity for heartless bullying and endangering others when they abandon Joseph in a pit to die and lead their father to believe that Joseph has been killed by a wild beast.

But even then, some rabbis disagree. Rabbi Judah ben Simon points out how the Hebrew Bible itself disapproves of Joseph's snitching by citing the Bible's literary justice. What goes around comes around as a repayment in kind for Joseph, who earns himself a mirror consequence for each piece of dirt he brings back. Accusing the brothers of eating limbs torn from living animals foreshadows the drenching of the coat of many colors in the blood of a goat. The allegation that some of his brothers taunt others as slaves foreshadows Joseph's sale into slavery. The claim of harassment of the local girls foreshadows Joseph's run-in with Potiphar's wife and her false accusation that Joseph made sexual advances (*Genesis Rabbah* 84:7).

Joseph learns a harsh lesson, that people will be furious when you go behind their backs and over their heads. As for their father, Jacob, he shows his poor parenting skills when he exacerbates the acrimony between his sons, instead of calming passions. Jacob sets off a sorrowful chain of events that leads to Joseph being thrown into that empty hole and all the tragic events that follow. Yet there is nobility to Joseph's truth telling; Joseph is honest about his brothers, to his detriment.

## Whistle-Blowing

You could call Joseph a "whistle-blower." A whistle-blower goes public, revealing inside information about something that is wrong. There could be a problem with a worker at the cash register who's outsmarting the computer system and pocketing the change. Maybe there are hazardous materials or poorly maintained machines in a factory that threaten worker safety or public health. Maybe a business keeps two sets of books, one hidden and the other for show. Or sexual harassment at the office might bring a whistle-blower forward in hopes that the harassment stops and justice is served. But before touting the moral imperative to come clean as a whistle with the noble truth, think twice, first. What happens to Joseph can happen to anyone else.

The matter is often open and shut when the rulebook rules, when a law or a professional code of conduct demands the reporting of suspected child or elder neglect or abuse, and there are often significant consequences for remaining silent, you have to speak up. These rules, in theory at least, take the decision out of individual hands. But what about times when the law makes no such demand? Then the person has to decide what to do on her own, and bad things can happen once the whistle gets blown.

Sounding the whistle can lead to being sued, fired, or jailed. You could be labeled a snitch, a stoolie, or a squealer. Whistle-blowers lose friends; ruin personal, professional, and business relationships; and have trouble finding other work. Of course, laws may protect whistle-blowers from retaliation, but even then, why deal with the risks of having your name dragged through the mud, years of litigation, and intense emotional pressure? And what if you accuse someone of wrongdoing and it turns out that he did nothing wrong? It may be better to keep quiet. But, saying nothing or leaving it to someone else to call it in means the problem may never go away. Silence can also turn potential whistle-blowers into accomplices, responsible for a problem that they did not even create.

It's often best to try to resolve the issue privately. Yet, merely raising a question about a supervisor or an associate puts a person at risk. What if you confide in someone who, it turns out, has a motive for keeping the secret a secret? What happens if that colleague or supervisor is a friend of the violator and unwilling to make trouble?

To be sure, with all the risk involved in whistle-blowing and other workplace moral dilemmas, there's also nobility. But deciding to tell the truth can be as complicated as deciding whether or not to lie, and sometimes a person has no choice. With this conversation on whistle-blowing in mind, we return to the Hebrew Bible and the story of the midwives serving under Pharaoh of Egypt, who defy a powerful leader's order and then lie about their insubordination.

## "The Hebrew Women Are Lively"

Pharaoh fears that a quickly expanding Jewish population will collaborate with the enemies of the state to overthrow him (Exodus 1:9–10). Pharaoh preemptively assigns the midwives Shifrah and Puah to enforce a harsh decree: the immediate death of all newborn Hebrew infant boys. But the midwives quietly disobey Pharaoh. According to the Talmud, "Not only did they keep the boys alive and spare them death; they made sure the infants had enough water and food (*Sotah* 11b). Pharaoh eventually learns that things are not happening according to instructions and called the midwives to explain why.

The rabbis are rightfully horrified by Pharaoh's strategy and respond by ridiculing him. "Whoever advised you to do this is an idiot!" they imagine themselves saying directly to Pharaoh in an allegorical time-warp fantasy. "You would be better off killing the girls. After all, without women, the men won't be able to marry. One woman cannot marry two men, but one man can marry ten or a hundred women" (*Exodus Rabbah* 1:14).

On the other hand, defending Pharaoh's logic while condemning his goals and behavior, one rabbi thinks Pharaoh hasn't lost his mind. Rabbi Hertz notes that girls "could not prove dangerous in time of war"; of course, Rabbi Hertz doesn't foresee women in combat. In another effort to get into Pharaoh's mind, Rabbi Yosi, son of Rabbi Hanina, says, "Pharaoh's astrologers told him, 'The mother of Israel's savior is already pregnant with him'" (*Exodus Rabbah* 1:18), leading Pharaoh to conclude that he had better do away with the soon-to-be-born Hebrew baby boy and eventual leader. Having no idea which boy will grow up to be the threat, Pharaoh decides to get rid of them all. In yet another interpretation, Pharaoh really means to say, "Let us do away with all the men so we may take the women for ourselves."[2] We can speculate on Pharaoh's motives, but at the end of the day, he assigns the midwives Shifrah and Puah to do the awful work, and the rabbis turn their eye to imagining the background of the women.

The Hebrew Bible's wording is unclear, leading a reader to guess whether they were "Hebrew midwives to the Hebrews" or "Egyptian midwives to the Hebrews." Assuming they were Hebrews, the rabbis say that Shifrah and Puah were Yoheved and Miriam, the mother and sister of Moses, respectively (Talmud, *Sotah* 11b). The Hebrew Bible calls Yoheved by the name Shifrah because she "straightened out" (*mishaperet* in Hebrew) the limbs of the newborn baby. Another rabbi says she was named Shifrah because the women of Israel were fruitful, *sheparu*, thanks to her work. The other midwife was named Puah because she "cried out," *poah*, and the child emerged (*Sotah* 11b), were it only that simple. Back to Rabbi Hertz, who insists they were Egyptian because Pharaoh couldn't possibly expect Hebrews to be so cruel to their own.[3]

Striking a similar note, Shadal and others wonder how "Pharaoh would order Jewish women to kill their own folk and imagine they would not divulge the whole plan" to other Hebrews.[4]

While there's disagreement over the midwives' backgrounds, there's no dispute about their bravery and courage. Pharaoh gets word that Hebrew boys are surviving, and he summons the midwives for questioning. "Oh, those Hebrew women are not like Egyptian women," Shifrah and Puah respond. "They are lively. They give birth before midwives can arrive" (Exodus 1:19). This is a lie and it takes courage. Fortunately for them, Pharaoh takes them at their word. What's more, this lie is no sin because God rewards it by literally "building up their houses" (Exodus 1:21). It's actually praiseworthy.

The midwives achieve a moral victory in addition to that compensation, because that noble lie puts them at personal risk and calls for great courage. Writes modern biblical scholar Nahum Sarna:

> Here we have history's first recorded case of civil disobedience in defense of a moral cause.... Faced with an irreconcilable conflict between obedience to the sovereign's depraved law and allegiance to the higher moral law of God, the midwives chose in favor of the transcendent imperative of morality.... What is remarkable is that the names of these ... women are recorded [by the Torah] whereas by contrast, the all-powerful reigning monarch is consistently veiled in anonymity. In this way the biblical narrator expressed his scale of values.[5]

There's the Hebrew Bible's sense of irony: It never mentions Pharaoh by name, leaving him anonymously buried in the heap of history. By contrast, the Hebrew Bible identifies the midwives by name for recognition through the generations.

Two very humble, hardworking women, serving 24/7 in obstetrics, get the better of their chief slave master and head of state.

All the power of the mighty Pharaoh, the outward magnifi-
cence of his realm, the dazzling splendor of his court, his
colossal monuments—are all illusory, ephemeral and in the
ultimate reckoning, insignificant, and they must crumble
into dust because they rest on foundations empty of moral
conduct.[6]

Pharaoh is outdone by two midwives. Of even greater significance,
the midwives bring Jewish history through a critical turning point.
Shifrah and Puah pivot the Hebrew Bible's narrative from enslavement to liberation, to the giving of the Torah at Sinai and the fulfillment of God's promise of life in the land of Canaan. The midwives
set the course of Jewish history.

## Lying to a Liar

The midwives lie to Pharaoh, and it's so very gratifying when an
evildoer tastes his own medicine. It's even more gratifying to be
the one to mete out the justice. It's the best schadenfreude there is.
But before taking this as a life lesson or appointing ourselves judge,
jury, and sheriff, it's important to ask whether a liar loses his right
to hear the truth just because he lies.

When considering lying to a liar, one first should question
what that lie is intended to accomplish. Is the goal to punish, retali-
ate, or get even? Is someone endangered or suffering, and will the
lie restore her to safety?

The rabbis are fine with lying to a crook, as we read in the
Talmud: "With an honest person, act honestly; and with a crooked
person act dishonestly" (II Samuel 22:7).

In another example, Rabbi Eliezer uses oblique language
to save himself. When arrested by the authorities on suspicion
of being a heretic, he offers up double-talk. The governor asks
why a wise person, like Rabbi Eliezer, would bother with Torah
study. Rabbi Eliezer replies, "I acknowledge the Judge as being

right," without specifying which judge he has in mind. The governor thinks that he is the "judge" Rabbi Eliezer is referring to. He spares Rabbi Eliezer, even though the rabbi really is pointing to the Higher Authority (Talmud, *Avodah Zarah* 16a–17b).

Yet sometimes lies are not punished with lies, and some sins aren't punished, either.

For instance, Joseph doesn't get back at his brothers for what they did to him; he toys with them, but he doesn't put them at risk the way they endangered him. Esau never takes revenge against Jacob, though he could have and it looked as if he would. To follow the range of the Hebrew Bible's examples, I don't have to respond to a liar with a lie or even respond at all.

There is plenty to consider before responding to a lie with a lie. First, just because something looks like a lie doesn't make it a lie. Did I hear correctly or did I misunderstand? Did the speaker honestly think it was the truth, only to speak without full knowledge of the facts at the time? If it was known to be a lie, is the liar about to apologize, and am I being so eager for payback that I beat that apology with a lie? So hold off a moment before lying to a liar. Take pause to consider asking for clarification before exacting retribution.

But let's say it was a lie, told by someone who should have known better. Let's say I tried to clear the air but failed. I considered other options, including a good kick in the pants, and now I decide that a telling a lie is the best response to the lie I have just been told. This sounds sensible, until we ask even more questions. How big a lie did I hear, and how big a lie does it deserve in return? How do I get just enough payback—not too much and not too little? Is there a truthful way to make my point? What's more, am I the best person to repay that lie in kind? Maybe someone else should tell it.

Retaliatory lying opens the possibility of escalating a conflict. Suppose the original liar catches me in my lie and lies again to me in response, and I return that lie with another lie, launching a Hatfield-McCoy kind of "lie feud," with each side getting back at the other. Or imagine that I lied inadvertently and was the first one of the two of us to lie; the whole thing started with me and I didn't even know it. Now, my counter-lie ups the ante; that's not noble at all. The point of all this, though, is that it makes sense to think things over before punishing a liar by telling a lie. As we note in the story of the Hebrew midwives in Egypt, we see a lie to a despotic taskmaster, told with the full authority of the Hebrew Bible behind them, so we can't rule out a lie to a liar, especially when the motivation for that lie is noble.

Part of this moral question is that I'm not Moses, Shifrah, or Puah, and neither are you. And the destiny of an entire suffering nation doesn't depend on my decisions alone or yours. While, thankfully, these extraordinary situations are rare, our midwives stand out. Their stories are an important part of what makes the Hebrew Bible a guide for us in our own lives.

## What We Have Seen

This little analysis of lying to liars brings a close to our information gathering. Now, we'll examine a Jewish approach to weighing truth and falsehood with an eye toward how we make our decisions every day.

To review before moving ahead, the little lie resembles the truth so much that in telling the little lie, we feel as if we're telling the truth. The little lie may include some truth while distorting or omitting other factors. It may start with the truth and then add a measure of untruthfulness to undermine any of its integrity. In addition, the little lie typically includes self-deception, evident in saying to oneself, "Oh, I can get away with it. No big deal. After all, it's only a little lie. It's so close to the truth that telling the little lie doesn't matter at all." The big lie, by contrast, generally lacks this element of self-deception. When it comes to the big lie, almost everyone agrees that this lie is a lie, be it a lie to protect or advance oneself, a lie intended to get someone else into trouble, or a noble lie that protects others at personal cost or risk.

A lie is not necessarily a sin, as we concluded when we saw some lies pass unnoticed, others rewarded, and some punished or repaid in kind. Just as the Hebrew Bible demands the truth, it also recognizes that there are times when serving the greater truth requires telling a lie that is, by comparison, smaller. So the Hebrew Bible and the rabbis approve of lying that covers social miscues, protects feelings and avoids embarrassment, or serves the peace. By contrast, the rabbis look unfavorably on lies told to avoid responsibility, lies to advance oneself at the expense of another, and lies intended to hurt others. We have considered a few examples of when a lie is expected, and we have finally seen the noble lie, a self-less lie intended to safeguard or advance the public good, typically told at great personal risk.

We worked under the assumption that each of our actions makes a difference. I believe that everything we do has an impact, whether or not we see that impact or are even aware of it. That may make this book seem, at times, overly fussy about the details. But I'm drawn to appreciate what has been called the "Butterfly Effect." The Butterfly Effect comes from the image of a butterfly flapping its wings in Africa contributing to a tornado in Texas. That's a pretty far-fetched consideration, of course, but no different than some of the hyperbole coming from the Torah or the rabbis. Yet, the Butterfly Effect holds true in the Hebrew Bible, when a few simple words from two humble midwives initiate a cascade of events that reaches historic proportions. The defiance of the mid-wives breaks the spell of enslavement and brings a positive turn for the people of Israel, making possible the redemption, freedom, and revelation. Like a butterfly in one place contributing to a major outcome someplace else, one sentence from two midwives makes all the difference.

As we continue with our final chapters, we can note that "honesty is the best policy," for sure, but that policy is filled with exceptions when it comes to the need to weigh fine distinctions. This fourth and final part of the book presents a framework for considering those distinctions. Back in chapter 7, our discussion about writing a letter of recommendation began the kind of analysis that a framework requires. Chapter 14 expands on that conversation. In it I reflect on my work in medical ethics and how free will affects moral agency. Finally, chapter 15 delves into how this discussion about personal decisions broadly informs Jewish living.

We're now ready to examine the Hebrew Bible's framework for deciding whether lying is appropriate and to explore one approach to living a distinctively Jewish life.

Part IV

# The Framework

# Chapter 13

# Instruments of Decision

In a scene Moses could never have imagined, I spent a couple hours on the Internet searching for editorial cartoons about lying, the kind of cartoons you'd see on a newspaper opinion page or in the *New Yorker*. I found more than anyone would care to count, cartoons poking fun at politicians lying to the public, salespeople lying to customers, spouses lying to each other, and more. For all the variety, the cartoons had one thing in common: an "all or nothing" or "binary" approach to what makes a lie a lie. There were no shades of gray. Regarding cartoon and caricature, the truth is always clear—humor requires clarity. But that binary outlook isn't very practical once we turn to reality. Life often demands more nuance than "true" or "false." We need a robust middle ground.

There may not be much to consider when it comes to deciding whether or not to pocket the extra twenty dollars at the cash register or when considering whether or not to add an inch of height to an Internet dating profile. We face many decisions like these every day, and it's not possible or reasonable to delve deeply into the moral implications of each one. And when people grapple with more complicated circumstances, no clergyperson, myself included, has a binary "catchall" to cover all the specifics of each situation. What's more, even if I knew what to do beyond a doubt, it would be wrong for me to impose my opinions on another person's life.

Nevertheless, a yes/no binary approach is often useful and appropriate in distinguishing right from wrong. The Hebrew Bible also provides clear-cut, unambiguous instructions regarding what is holy or profane, kosher or not, or when a leader faces a significant decision about the direction in which to lead the nation.

The book of Exodus describes the High Priest's garments, a multicolored uniform with a breastplate containing the *urim* and *tumim*, also known as the "instruments of decision" (Exodus 28:15). We don't know what the instruments of decision looked like, what they were made of, or how they were used. Maybe they were dice, sticks, or stones that gave their decision after being shaken, tossed, and thrown to the ground. All we can say is that when the leader of Israel faces a difficult problem, he turns to the High Priest, who consults the *urim* and *tumim* for guidance. The *urim* and *tumim* provide a "yes" or "no" response, and that is that. There sure are times when I wish I had those instruments of decision to make up my mind for me.

The Hebrew Bible gives us a simple thumbs-up or thumbs-down regarding what we eat and the holidays we observe; it also recognizes that life circumstances create situations that deserve much more than a quick answer. The people of the Hebrew Bible grapple with complicated problems, such as the disappearance of family members, a disagreement over an inheritance, or a job description that goes well beyond the bounds of what a midwife, in her heart, believes to be good and right. No quick-acting instrument of decision could properly address these challenging circumstances. Fortunately, the Hebrew Bible and the rabbis study these situations and offer us a framework for reaching respectful and compassionate decisions. We don't have that breastplate with the pocket anymore; we have the Hebrew Bible itself as our guide and support. Let's take a couple of examples to see what makes this appreciation for nuance so important and consider some of the problems that arise when we don't have a more refined measure.

# The Nose and the Meter

Everything is great when the storybook-turned-cartoon-character Pinocchio tells the truth, but his nose grows longer whenever he lies. Pinocchio's nose is a true-false lie detector, a "binary" yes/no gauge that grows the same amount each time Pinocchio lies, no matter what kind of lie he tells. Like the *urim* and *tumim*, the nose knows no gradations. To be sure, Pinocchio, like a philosopher facing an involved set of circumstances, can spend an entire day boiling down a dilemma to a hierarchy of simplistic true-false questions, put them to a nose test, and see which ones fly. But even if he can get this strategy to work, he's still left to deal with that nose going on overload over the "Pinocchio Paradox."

The Pinocchio Paradox imagines Pinocchio saying, "My nose grows now" while his nose is growing. Now, the nose should not be growing, since he is telling the truth. But if it stops growing, it turns him into a liar, so it should grow anyway. The Pinocchio Paradox, like any other paradox, is a mental twister that takes a few simple words to claim that two contradictory things are impossibly true, both at the same time. Pinocchio's nose is unable to determine whether the Pinocchio Paradox is true or not, showing that when it comes to discerning the fine points, the nose isn't a useful yardstick, not at all. Before getting too serious, let's stay in this lighter voice with a slightly more refined measure called the "Truth-O-Meter."

The PolitiFact "Truth-O-Meter"[1] rates statements made by public officials as "True," "Mostly True," "Half True," "Mostly False," or "False," with the most egregious fabrications earning the lowest score of "Pants on Fire." Unlike Pinocchio's nose, the Truth-O-Meter recognizes some shades of difference. The Truth-O-Meter may be useful when a voter is deciding how to cast a ballot. But this informal measuring tool falls short when there's a need for finer shades.

In a world where simple questions raise multiple concerns and cause multiple impacts, we need more than a yes/no, true/false/mostly false instrument of decision. We need more nuance, the kind of thinking that the Hebrew Bible and the rabbis provide.

## The Prism

Passing light through a glass prism sends a rainbow of different colors out the other side. In the same way, we place a prism on the Hebrew Bible and are graced by a colorful spectrum of ideas. For example, Abraham and Sarah's "spouse-sibling" story raises an array of issues regarding Abraham's integrity, Sarah's well-being, the nature of their relationship, the future of the Jewish people, the role of God, the propriety of falsehood when life is at risk, as well as a lie—of deception, or at least omission—that the Hebrew Bible sees rewarded. That spectrum of ideas speaks to how we live our lives, too. The Hebrew Bible, as interpreted by our rabbis, is our instrument of decision, leading us to a Jewish framework for deciding.

This framework is not a rulebook, but a snapshot of Jewish principles that lead to thinking and living in Jewish ways. This framework gives us an approach to life. It highlights key considerations without delving into every aspect of every situation. What's more, I'm not interrogating you; you ask these questions of yourself, without me holding you to account. I'll often make judgments or express opinions, but let's remember that I'm not the boss of your life; you are. You are the one to decide.

So you can ask these questions to build that Jewish framework:

- What if I told the truth?

- Is a law or a code of ethics involved?

- Have I considered a test of publicity?

- Am I prepared to take responsibility?

- Am I under duress?

- How would I feel if someone lied to me like that?

- After the fact: Do I express repentance and ask forgiveness?

# The Framework

## What If I Told the Truth?

As we discussed earlier, begin building a personal moral framework by asking "What if?" That is to say, "What if I told the truth?"

What if the brothers owned up to abandoning Joseph in a pit? What if Abraham told Sarah where he was taking Isaac before they left or if Rebecca was more up front about the wisdom in having Isaac bless Jacob instead of Esau? A Jewish framework would have us put the truth on the table for personal, private consideration beforehand, even when there is absolutely no chance it is going to be told, even when it's absolutely clear that lying is the most moral and practical thing to do.

Asking yourself "What if I told the truth?" means being honest about lying and avoiding self-deception. Saying, "I could have told the truth, but I decided against it and said what I said instead," ensures that only one lie is told, not two. That is to say, "I'm lying to someone else, but I am being honest with myself." The Hebrew Bible sets a good model of candor by being truthful even when its favorite characters aren't.

Honesty when lying also puts that lie in a Jewish context, on the spiritual agenda for Shabbat and the High Holy Days, the times when Judaism has us ask ourselves, "Where did I fall short? What can I do to fix the situation I created? What will be different next time?" Above all, starting with the truth may lead a person to go ahead and tell the truth, and that may not be such a bad thing, not at all. So honoring the teaching "Keep far from falsehood" is a good place to start.

## Is a Law or a Code of Ethics Involved?

After asking, "What if I told the truth?" go on to ask, "Are any laws or professional obligations at stake?"

### THE LAW OF THE LAND

Perjury laws ensure honesty in the courtroom. Business laws require honesty about quality when selling meat, nuts, or a can of soup. The Internal Revenue Service expects accurate reporting of income and prohibits overstatement of deductions. Privacy laws forbid medical professionals from giving out patient information without that individual's permission. When a social worker, doctor, or teacher working in a professional capacity believes someone is guilty of child abuse or elder neglect, state laws typically mandate reporting to the authorities. When it comes to doing right and speaking truthfully, unless you're the equivalent of a midwife in Pharaoh's Egypt and in a situation like hers, legal requirements trump the moral demands when there's a duty to disclose the truth. What's more, Judaism has long affirmed that "the law of the land is the law."

### WORKPLACE AND PROFESSIONAL DECISIONS

An employee handbook regulates workplace behavior. A code of ethics provides for sanction or expulsion from a professional organization when a member commits an act of sexual misconduct, or it requires reporting an "impaired colleague"—for instance, turning in a colleague suspected of working under the influence of drugs or alcohol. Codes of ethics also underscore the rules that govern the professions, as they also encourage taking informal consultation from colleagues when a professional faces a complicated situation and is unsure about what to do.

## Have I Considered a Test of Publicity?

As we saw in chapter 7, a "test of publicity" is one of the most important and effective moral and Jewish tools we have. According to the Talmud, "Rabbi Kahanah said, "When a fact will ... come to light, people don't lie about it" (*Rosh Hashanah* 22b), wisely cautioning us to ask, "What if my lie is discovered?" These days, with our electronic communication and record keeping, it is becoming harder to keep things private. In our times, more than ever, considering "What if this lie is discovered?" can clarify how to behave in a muddy, fast-moving situation.

Joseph put Potiphar's wife's proposal to the test of publicity, suggesting to her:

> "I'm afraid of my master." She said to him, "I'll murder him." Joseph said to her, "It is not enough to be in the company of adulterers, but in the company of murderers." (*Genesis Rabbah* 87:5)

Too bad for Joseph that this doesn't work.

It makes sense to assume that a secret or mistruth will come to light. I'll often advise that "there are no secrets, especially in a family." Besides, even if you are able to hide the truth, that successful concealment comes at the cost of worry that the truth will become known. As the often-repeated saying goes, "Always tell the truth. That way, you don't have to remember what you said."

## Am I Prepared to Take Responsibility?

We said that every lie has a double effect, one that's often unanticipated. Adam and Eve don't expect that eating the fruit of the Tree of Knowledge of Good and Evil will get them thrown out of Eden. Looking more deeply at Sarah's and Abraham's decision to lie about their marriage, we see that their misrepresentation almost costs King Abimelech his life. Joseph never imagines that his boasting and tattling will land him at the bottom of a pit. Everything we do has multiple impacts. Plan all you want for unforeseen fallout, but many outcomes will surprise the most prepared liar and truth teller. The reality is that no one knows what consequences our actions will bring about.

Will a lie protect someone from harm? Will it advance a person's career? Will it stave off blame, responsibility, or punishment? Will a lie mitigate financial loss, embarrassment, or emotional distress? Who will the lie impact—the teller or the listener or a third party? Will it serve the well-being of a nation or save a life, or will the lie simply feed a need to make the liar feel vindicated?

People disagree about the role of intention and results, whether the speaker is responsible for all the consequences or just the ones that can be foreseen, even when a lie works for the good. The Hebrew Bible repeatedly demonstrates the need to be aware of a gaping distance between expectation and reality, between intention and what actually happens. It makes sense to assume that the double effect is in play and that, as far as I can see in the Hebrew Bible, I must take all the responsibility for the consequences— anticipated or not—of what I do.

When something unexpected happens, it's all too tempting to shirk responsibility and blame someone else. When God asks about the fruit of the Tree of Knowledge, Adam blames eating the fruit on Eve, she blames the snake, and God rejects these attempts to wiggle out and evade. Rebecca encourages Jacob to get beyond his misgivings and impersonate Esau by insisting that the liability will be hers; the Hebrew Bible will have none of that. The Hebrew Bible holds each of us to account as individuals. When it comes to answering for our behavior, we alone shoulder the responsibility for our actions.

## Am I Under Duress?

Judaism accepts—even encourages—a lie told to protect or save life during a public crisis like a famine. But what about lying to head off a less significant threat, like driving away from a fender-bender you caused but no one saw without leaving your contact information or lying to a judge about the circumstances surrounding a speeding ticket? All these situations are "stressful." Nevertheless, the upsetting circumstances surrounding a bashed car bumper differs, in large ways, from a life-threatening situation.

Emotional duress is not necessarily an adequate excuse for shading the truth.

So, a crisis in and of itself doesn't automatically justify lying. It's the difference between saying, "I lied because I was under pressure," and saying, "I looked at the situation and realized that a lie could achieve something worthwhile, so I lied. And by the way, it was a very stressful situation." Fortunately, life-threatening circumstances like those chronicled in the Hebrew Bible are rare.

### How Would I Feel If Someone Lied to Me Like That?

Mentioning the Golden Rule brings up that old debate as to which religion has the better version. Hillel says, "What is hateful to you, do not do to your neighbor" (Talmud, *Shabbat* 31a), while Jesus says, "Do to others as you would want them to do to you" (Matthew 7:12). Both these teachings grew out of "Love your neighbor as yourself" (Leviticus 19:18), and arguing over semantics misses the larger point: the Golden Rule is good advice, so let's not get sidetracked by engaging in religious squabbling. When it comes to truth telling, the issue is very simple. It's in asking the question, "How would I feel if someone spoke to me the way I am about to speak to someone else?"

## After the Fact: Repentance and Forgiveness

Judaism gives us ways to consider our deeds, make amends, learn from our errors, and move on—but only after the fact. Excuse me for being preachy here, but this is not "I'll fudge my answer, say a few prayers, and then I'll be good to go with God." Instead, the Hebrew Bible expects heartfelt examination both beforehand and afterward. It's about doing all that spiritual work up front and all the way through.

Weighing serious matters of truth and falsehood calls for soulful consideration. It relies on asking what would happen after a lie is told and the truth comes out. That includes paying close attention to what an action is expected to achieve. It requires a willingness to accept personal responsibility for the action, whatever the outcome. Finally, it includes honest questioning of how we would feel if the tables were turned and the speaker became the target of the lie. At the end of the day, we each have to make up our own minds and live with the consequences of what we decide to do.

My previous book, *All Politics Is Religious* (SkyLight Paths Publishing), describes a cartoon of a distraught preschool student in one of those tiny chairs at a table full of toys. The caption reads, "Do we have to do what we want to do?" With so many options, it's hard to decide.

Yes, it's tough to decide, whether you're a nursery-school student or an adult. Nevertheless, when this book asks the question "Do we *have* to do what we want to do?" the answer is "Yes! You must!" No one else can make up your mind for you; no one else will live with the consequences of a situation that you create for yourself. You are your own instrument of decision.

Jewish decision making relies on two sources of truth—the truth we learn from the Hebrew Bible and the rabbis, alongside the truth we learn by living. We acquire the truth of the Hebrew Bible through Jewish learning, seen in the reaction of "Aha!" when an insight from the Hebrew Bible makes a difference in what we think or how we live. We also learn from life experience.

The next chapter will explore my learning from personal life experience when I worked in the field of medical ethics.

## Chapter 14

# Medical Ethics: Personal Decisions and Jewish Perspectives

I came to medical ethics while serving as the rabbi of a congregation in rural New England, and the patient care ethics committee of the local hospital invited me to become a member. The ethics committee included experts in law, mental health, and a variety of medical specialties and callings, as well as clergy from differing faiths.

When a situation came before the committee, we heard out the concerns of those involved, including doctors, nurses, other health care workers, patients, and their family members. We questioned, listened, and often advised, but we never dictated. We recommended but never imposed or coerced. We didn't reward and we didn't punish. We encouraged consideration of reasonable legal and practical options, and sometimes a recommendation was based solely on what the law said. All our deliberations affirmed that the person seeking our counsel was the one responsible for deciding.

The patient, in some small way, resembled our undecided nursery-school student, surrounded by all those toys. The patient had the final responsibility to sort through all the options before choosing which course of action to pursue. For all the wisdom in the old saying that "the doctor knows best," we also recognized that the best doctors know that the patient plays a critical role in setting the course of treatment. To be sure, a doctor is morally obligated to refuse to provide a treatment that won't cure or bring comfort. But, when push came to shove, we knew that the patient had the right—the responsibility, really—to decide what is to be done with her body when it came to choosing or refusing a treatment.

Assuming that you and I are not medical professionals, we'll invariably find it frustrating to have a complicated health decision foisted on us, especially when medical testing is inconclusive, options are limited, and no course of action is ideal. It's natural and understandable to try to defer to the doctor. After all, the doctor is the expert and has the information, experience, and wisdom to set the direction. In the end, however, health care providers recommend, encourage, and sometimes even nag, but the patient makes the final decision.

As members of the patient care ethics committee, we dealt with a range of issues, from a religious prohibition against a blood transfusion to a family member wanting a loved one to receive treatment that would not bring any medical benefit, and more. We worked together as an interdisciplinary team to address disagreement when values conflicted, or when a patient considered the risks and possible benefits of an experimental treatment, when a new medical resident needed to figure out how to care for a non-communicating patient, when a nurse was flummoxed by a patient refusing the most effective treatment, or when a patient behaved in a physically threatening way that challenged staff to get close enough to provide care without themselves getting hurt. As you might imagine, questions about the direction of end-of-life care took up most of our time.

An advanced-care directive is often helpful when a patient becomes unable to make his wishes known. An advanced-care directive gives written instructions regarding medication, comfort measures, and what to do about heroic medical treatments that may or may not prolong life. The advanced-care directive is different from a "proxy." A health care proxy is not a paper, but a person—a spouse, a relative, or a good friend who knows a person well enough to anticipate what that person, left unable to speak for himself, would likely say.

Sometimes people leave no instructions, forcing the health care team and family or friends, if any, to figure out what to do. But even when the advanced-care directive and health care proxy are in place, it may be difficult to determine a patient's wishes in an unforeseen, rare, or extremely complicated medical situation. Even with advance planning, a disagreement within a heath care team or among family members raises important concerns. Or, a proxy or doctor might claim that the written directive is outdated, that the patient had since changed his mind about his care plan and never got around to putting new instructions in writing. In cases like those, the committee provided support for care that everyone involved thought the patient would want. A patient care ethics committee serves as a valuable resource in these situations.

As you might expect, when a patient was unable to communicate and the direction for care was unclear, our committee deliberations turned to that one question: "What would the patient have wanted?" This wasn't about what the doctor wanted to do or what a patient's friend or relative thought would be good, or what anyone in the patient's social circle believed to be in the patient's best interests. We focused on what is called "substituted judgment"—that is to say, it meant figuring out what the patient would have wanted. Imagine yourself in the patient's situation—what choice would she make for herself?

We arrived at that substituted judgment through questions, like these:

- If the patient knew about this situation, what would he want to see done?

- What did she say when others were in situations like this one?

- How did his parents or other loved ones die? Did he ever comment on that?

- Did she ever say anything about a friend in a situation like this?

- When there was a TV show or a news story about someone with a serious medical condition, how did he react?

Again, the individual knows herself best, and we were usually strangers to the patient. Besides, none of us had to live with the consequences of the decision. At heart, though, we recognized that we are each expert in one thing—ourselves. The decision rests with the individual.

When I'm approached by a Jewish person about these matters, I first respond with Jewish perspectives to provide a traditional religious framework for reaching an informed Jewish decision.[1] But when I am working with an interfaith and interdisciplinary team, other factors come into play.

While the specifics of proxies and advance-care directives vary from state to state, medical ethics is governed by the values of beneficence, nonmalfeasance, justice, and autonomy. Beneficence speaks to the responsibility to provide care and comfort that honors the well-being of the patient. Nonmalfeasance means to "do no harm." Justice refers to the imperative that each of us should have access to the care that we and our health care provider believe we need. Autonomy in medicine means that the patient is told and understands his medical situation and treatment options, appreciates the intended benefits and risks of each option, and understands what happens if nothing is done.

As I discussed in my previous book, *All Politics Is Religious* (SkyLight Paths Publishing), making a personal, private decision about faith, health care, or anything else has everything to do with the Hebrew Bible. At the end of the day, the experience serving as an instructor of medical ethics and a member of a patient care ethics committee deepened my understanding of and appreciation for the need to respect the process of decision making that speaks to the exercise of what we call "free will," "conscience," "moral agency," or "autonomy" of the individual.

# The Hebrew Bible and Personal Decisions

The Jewish respect for individual decision making begins with the story of the Tree of Knowledge of Good and Evil in the Garden of Eden. When we considered this story earlier, we saw what happens when the truth is embellished. Now we come to the main point of the experience in Eden, one that is central to the Hebrew Bible and Jewish living, and one that has everything to do with our godlike capacity to exercise spiritual freedom.

Erich Fromm, the twentieth-century German-born Jewish psychoanalyst, sociologist, and progressive writer, drew from his deep Jewish roots to craft a positive approach to human nature, resting largely on the experience of Adam and Eve in Eden. In contrast to those who see the "fall" from Eden as a punishment and evidence of human sinfulness, Fromm, like many Jewish teachers, underscores the lessons of freedom in the story.

It is wrong and a sin to defy God by eating the fruit. Yet that act of rebellion gives human beings the godlike ability to make decisions, just as the name of the tree says. Their act of defiance enables them to weigh fine distinctions, live out their convictions, and bear the responsibility for their actions. In Fromm's classic book *You Shall Be as Gods*, he says of the Eden experience, "This is not the story of the 'fall' of man but of his awakening, and thus, of the beginning of his rise."[2] The Eden story is a "Just So" explanation of how we became as smart as we are.

Fromm follows Jewish teachers, like Rashi, who consider that "the eyes of both of them were opened" in the Eden story. As Rashi points out:

> Scripture speaks here about wisdom, not about actually seeing. As the verse continues, "They realized they were naked." Even a blind person realizes that they are naked.[3]

Rashi encourages us to take this incident as metaphor. This isn't about sex or eyesight, and it isn't a fashion statement. It is about our ability to decide, something at the center of the human soul. Eating that fruit opens their eyes to determining the good and the truth.

It might be tempting to dismiss Fromm as just another unrealistic idealist. After all, how can anyone speak of people as moral or trustworthy after the Holocaust? The reality is that Fromm knew what he was talking about from personal experience. He fled Nazi Germany for the United States in 1934, and he understood that people will make bad personal decisions, decisions that even they acknowledge are bad for them. They choose paths that you and I would not take for ourselves. As Fromm witnessed, the reality is that, short of using force, which we had to do against the Nazis, there is very little we can do in such situations. Fromm recognizes that people will fall from the ideal, yet he challenges us to respect freedom, as we learn from the story of Eden and through other examples of discernment and responsibility in the Hebrew Bible.

## Choosing the Right Path

Fromm bases many of his ideas on the story of the Garden of Eden, and the Hebrew Bible contains other examples of respect for personal decision making. The very next chapter of Genesis, following the expulsion from Eden, tells how Cain and Abel offer sacrifices to God. Abel, the shepherd, brings an offering from the best of his flock, and God accepts Abel's offer. Cain, the farmer, brings produce, and God rejects Cain's. After all, as the rabbis point out, Cain offers second-rate produce. Says Rashi, "*The fruit of the earth*: The worst fruits."[4]

While God wants nothing of Cain's gift, God speaks encouragingly to Cain:

> Why are you so angry?
> Why your fallen face?
> Surely, if you do well, there will be uplift.
> But if you do not do well

> Sin crouches at the door.
> Its urge is to you,
> But you can rule over it. (Genesis 4:6–7)

Like a coach giving a discouraged team member a pep talk, God reassures Cain that improvement is well within his reach. Yet Cain is unmoved, spurns God's words, remains jealous of Abel, and goes on to take his rage out on his brother by murdering him. Cain makes a bad decision. He pursues the sin "at the door" and suffers the rest of his life.

As in the Cain and Abel story, each person wrestles with powerful and conflicting inclinations—a *yetzer tov*, an inclination to do good, and a *yetzer rah*, an inclination to do evil. Judaism also teaches that it is up to the individual to ensure that the *yetzer tov* wins out over the *yetzer rah*, so that life advances in a positive direction.

The book of Deuteronomy gives additional examples of how God leaves decisions to us and hopes we make wise ones, but God can only hope. What we decide to do is beyond God's control.

> May they always be like this, that their hearts be like this, to revere Me and keep all My commandments. (Deuteronomy 5:26)

The Hebrew Bible speaks as if God knows we have free will and prays that we do right. Later on in Deuteronomy, God reiterates that hope for us:

> See, I have set before you this day life and good, death and evil. That is, I am commanding you today to love the Eternal your God, to walk in God's ways, and keep God's commandments, laws, and rules so that you live, grow in number, and the Eternal, your God, blesses you in the land that you are entering to possess. (Deuteronomy 30:15–16)

## The Hebrew Bible: Free Will Denied

As we have seen earlier, there are times when the Hebrew Bible seems to contradict itself. Just as God grants us freedom, God takes freedom away, especially from those who would harm us. The book of Exodus holds the outstanding example, when God "hardens" Pharaoh's heart as a pretext for inflicting the ten plagues (Exodus 4:21).

This incident is guaranteed to spark animated conversation at Torah study. We struggle with the fairness of God's action: How could a God of justice hold people accountable for their actions when there is no option other than to sin? A punishment, like the ten plagues, is only fair when people are free to decide and act on their decisions—it's not right to take free will away, force people to do wrong, and then punish them when they have no other choice. How could God punish Pharaoh after leaving him no alternative but to be defiant?

My advice is to take this situation as an outlier, the exception. As much as the Hebrew Bible is committed to free will, it just isn't very concerned about the few times that God denies that free will. The Hebrew Bible wants to set the stage for the ten plagues by showcasing God's strength and dominion. In other words, God gives us free will, except every now and then when God doesn't, and the Hebrew Bible doesn't seem to worry too much about that. This story is one example of how our Jewish ideals have evolved over time; that idea made sense to someone long ago, just as we struggle with it today. Yet, as we discussed earlier, the truth in the story of the ten plagues has to do with the wonder and the timing of natural events that appear to be miraculous, the need to care for our planet earth, and the necessity for human freedom.

Yet, before we move on, we should note that God denies free will to other enemies of Israel as well. Moses reflects on our history and recalls that when we are wandering in the wilderness, "The king of Sihon of Heshbon would not let us pass through there because God stiffened his spirit and hardened his heart so God would turn them over to you, as today" (Deuteronomy 2:30). And in another example, one regarding the Canaanites: "God hardened their heart to war with Israel" (Joshua 11:20). So, for all the times we assert the importance of free will in Judaism, we have to acknowledge the small handful of times when the people—specifically, our enemies— just don't receive it. Again, this is one illustration—a challenging one, to be sure—of the way Jewish ideas grow over time, but not in a straight line. We accept some beliefs, reject others, and hold conflicting thoughts at the same time. Judaism evolves during the days of the Hebrew Bible, as it continues to evolve in our time, too.

Of course, Judaism has much more to teach about free will. In another example, the Mishnah says that God knows the outcome of our decisions, but God's foreknowledge has no impact on how or what we decide. As we read, "Everything is foreseen, yet permission is given" (*Avot* 3:15). And the Talmud tells us that "everything is in the hand of heaven, except the fear of heaven" (*Berachot* 33b). The rabbis appreciate God who sees things in advance, on the one hand, and grants free will, on the other.

In a more contemporary setting, leaders of Reform Judaism have long held that "Jewish obligation begins with the informed will of the individual" and call on us "to confront the claims of Jewish tradition, however differently perceived, and to exercise their individual autonomy, choosing and creating on the basis of commitment and knowledge."[5] We "inform" the "will" through Jewish learning and life experience, and then we use that "will" by exercising good judgment. This statement illustrates the expectation that we learn what Judaism teaches and then consider those ancient teachings in light of modern thinking and personal experience with the goal of arriving at a considered conclusion.

So the Hebrew Bible values personal decision making, just as the rabbis and more contemporary commentators do. Now let's see how that free will applies more broadly and deeply to Jewish life.

# Chapter 15

# A Rulebook for Living or a Framework for Deciding?

## Same Candles, Same Prayers

As a young student in an Orthodox yeshiva, I learned the importance of lighting Shabbat candles at the precise moment before sunset each Friday evening when Shabbat begins. As my family migrated to Reform Judaism, I saw Shabbat candles lit at 8:30 p.m. at services in the synagogue sanctuary each Friday evening, week after week, regardless of when the sun set or what my Orthodox teachers said. Where the Orthodoxy of my childhood took a right/wrong "binary" approach to this Jewish practice, the Reform Judaism of my later growing-up years had a very different outlook. Reform Judaism found meaning through welcoming Shabbat as a community, together. Same candles, challah, and wine, all to the same prayers, but with the underlying logic making all the difference. In exploring this difference further, my teacher Rabbi Eugene Borowitz of the Hebrew Union College–Jewish Institute of Religion

140

compared two Jewish works: the sixteenth-century, multivolume Jewish legal code the *Shulhan Aruch* and *The Jewish Catalog: A Do-It-Yourself Kit*[1] of the 1970s.

Sixteenth-century scholar Rabbi Joseph Caro compiled the *Shulhan Aruch*, literally "a set table," a multivolume rulebook written with the goal of standardizing Jewish religious practice for the dispersed and divided Jewish communities of his day. In an era of startling Jewish differences from country to country, the *Shulhan Aruch* "set the table" with specific instructions for keeping kosher, conversion to Judaism, observance of holidays, and much more. While Caro had his critics, the *Shulhan Aruch* had a landmark influence on Jewish development.

By contrast, *The Jewish Catalog* grew to a three-volume set to offer twentieth-century Jews a framework, a collection of traditions and rituals for enriching Jewish life as they individually saw fit. *The Jewish Catalog* wasn't too concerned about uniformity. It was an invitation to customize Judaism in a personally meaningful way. Where the *Shulhan Aruch* gave us a rulebook, *The Jewish Catalog* provided a framework.

*The Jewish Catalog* addresses the perception that Judaism is dreary, stale, and inflexible. It speaks in joyous voice and offers an array of traditional options, suggesting without insisting, recommending without prescribing, trusting individuals to make wise, personal choices within Jewish parameters. It emphasizes individual participation, speaks warmly, and presents it all in an accessible format to encourage positive Jewish identity and living.

The *Shulhan Aruch* expects each and every Jew to live by each one of those recorded rules, exactly as written. By contrast, *The Jewish Catalog* provides an array of traditional options, so a person can identify and perform those found to be personally meaningful. This marriage of Jewish tradition and heartfelt ritual practice strengthens the Jewish people. The very act of delegating religious authority to the individual is engaging and empowering. It sparks Jewish learning and builds Jewish commitment by making people self-directing and self-responsible. It strengthens the bonds of Jewish communal life.

So you welcome Shabbat by lighting candles and blessing the wine and the challah. Does that make you Orthodox, or are you something else? It's the same candles, wine, and challah, and the same Hebrew prayers, whatever denomination you are, if any. The difference is in how a person comes to these practices, either through the decision to accept a set table of Jewish living or a decision to accept a practice from a range of Jewish options. There's decision making either way, and decision making is one thing that all Jews have in common. With all the talk these days about religious differences, when it comes to making decisions, we have reached Jewish common ground.

## A Framework Begins with Learning

As noted above, authentic Jewish decisions begin with historical Jewish teaching; no branch of Judaism is "anything goes." You don't have to be an expert in Judaism to have a Jewish opinion, but a Jewish opinion should be informed by Jewish teaching. Starting with a Jewish framework means beginning with Jewish knowledge and study. It all rests on an understanding of and respect for the beliefs and practices of Jews who lived before us as well as what Jews do today.

For example, when I meet with a couple to discuss a wedding, I'll start by describing a Jewish ceremony, including the huppah (the Jewish wedding canopy), the *ketubah* (the Jewish marriage contract), and other traditional elements and rituals. Then I'll describe what other people typically do and ask for feedback. The point is that we begin with Jewish practice and then talk about what they believe is right for them.

So we would be mistaken to say that "Reform Judaism lets you do whatever you want." That "anything goes" picture is a mischaracterization. The reality is that Reform Judaism expects each of us to do the spiritual work of seeking out the most truthful personal Jewish path and living it. To be sure, Jews from all walks of belief and practice fall short of these expectations—we have Orthodox Jews who make up their own minds, just as we do in other denominations, and there is not much any of us should or can do about this. After all, religion is a voluntary activity. You can't force a person to have faith; you can't force anyone to reject her beliefs or live by someone else's. But, if you want to know what authentic Jewish living is all about, it begins with Jewish teaching, which leads to the heartfelt deliberation that drives Jewish action.

## A Framework Leads to Action

While many faiths pride themselves on answering all your questions, I find that Torah study often feels like a place where "all your answers are questioned," and that's a positive aspect of Jewish communal living that I welcome. While we deliberate and question, the most important point of all this is that we eventually do something. All that talking and thinking have to lead to action. Turning inward should bring a soul to eventually turn outward. Action is essential to faith.

Just as Jewish living includes Jewish learning, it also includes Jewish community. Twentieth-century Austrian psychiatrist and writer Viktor Frankl has been called the "doctor of the soul" and was known for his landmark book *Man's Search for Meaning*. Frankl chronicled his experience as a concentration camp prisoner during the Nazi Holocaust. Among his many teachings, he said that "the door to the spirit opens outward." The full life is lived in relationship with others and in the larger world.

Jewish living also "opens outward" into relationship, in engagement with the tradition, the Jewish community, the Land of Israel, and the larger Jewish people. Eugene Borowitz adds to Frankl's thinking when he says:

In Jewish belief, the self cannot be the exclusive object of its primary concern. Its meaning is very largely given it by its relations with others. We are true persons, in the Jewish view, only as we fulfill our responsibilities to those with whom we live. Because we are historical creatures, we necessarily are obliged to those who came before us and those who will follow after us.[2]

The key word here is "exclusive." Judaism isn't asking us for extreme self-sacrifice or self-deprivation. Rather, the Hebrew Bible points to the enduring satisfaction that comes from turning outward. Self-satisfaction comes to a person as a by-product of being in relationship with others.

## Welcoming Diversity

People worry that an emphasis on personal religious responsibility threatens the stability and integrity of the Jewish people. After all, if each of us arrives at differing conclusions, then Jewish communities will be diverse, leading some to warn that we will fall into disorganization and anarchy. The reality is that we are already very varied. Just look at the variety of Jewish life in Israel or across the neighborhoods of New York City, for instance. Besides, as already mentioned, religion is voluntary, so we can't realistically legislate one Jewish standard into the private lives of others. What is more, differing Jewish approaches ensure Jewish continuity, just as diversity has served us well throughout history. We can't be entirely sure of which Jewish perspective will continue to flourish. The more options we have, the more secure our future.

## All Movements Have Expectations

Some Jews expect us all to believe that the world is not even six thousand years old. They require men to dress one way and expect

Yiddish to be spoken at home, to the exclusion of English, Hebrew, or other languages. In other denominations, like mine, we ordain women, welcome same-gender individuals and couples into our communities as members and leaders, and when it comes to understanding how the earth came to be, expect science-based education for our kids—those are our expectations. As in more "traditional" denominations, my synagogue prohibits the serving of shellfish and pork, encourages the observance of Shabbat and the festivals, and recognizes that the High Holy Day season calls for self-evaluation. All branches of Judaism have expectations and make demands. This points to the reality that Jews across denominations have more in common with each other than we differ. Rather than build or expand wedges, it's important to bridge differences, to focus on what brings us together.

## Epilogue

# The Examined
# Jewish Life

It's been quite some time since I read *Lying* by Sissela Bok and saw the Torah through that lens. All these years later, with all the time I've spent learning, thinking, and teaching, and more recently, writing, the better part of me still wants to hear the Hebrew Bible say that every lie is a sin and that each of our spiritual ancestors follows that teaching to the letter. But the Hebrew Bible doesn't say any of that, and what's more, just about everyone in the Hebrew Bible lies. All this adds up to the conclusion that we should always be honest and avoid lying until telling a lie is the most moral option, as, sooner or later, it will surely become. This mixed moral message is not unique to our Hebrew Bible. Leaders from all walks of life, including sports figures, entertainers, religious leaders, and international figures, all deal with the same concerns as the rest of us. That's certainly true of the founders and early leaders of the United States.

You recall the legend of young George Washington and the cherry tree, of course. George receives a hatchet as a gift from his dad, and like a child with a new toy—which George and his gift literally were—he chops down everything in sight, including his father's favorite and legendary English cherry tree. When confronted by his angry father, George hesitates but responds with the

146

famous words "I cannot tell a lie" and prepares to accept the consequences of his action. George's father, so taken by George's honesty, calms down and decides not to punish George.

You probably won't get your kid a gift of a hatchet anytime soon. More likely, that present has a plug that goes into an outlet in the wall. But the point of this legend is that many people assume that there was a time when our national leaders were born honest and brought that honesty to their offices. That's the way it was in the good old days, when integrity and politics supposedly went hand in hand. Yet the story of a youngster who grows up to be president, standing up to receive his punishment by proclaiming, "I cannot tell a lie," is nothing more than a story—it's all made up.

As yet another story goes, President Washington's biographer, Parson Weems, concocted the cherry tree legend in 1809, a decade after President Washington's death.[1] "Pants on fire!" to Mr. Weems.

Then there was President Abraham Lincoln, Honest Abe. Speaking—in real life—to the New Jersey State Senate in 1861, President Lincoln describes himself as a "humble instrument in the hands of the Almighty, and of this, His almost chosen people."[2] He knows who and what he is made of; no pretenses for him. And he calls us Americans "almost chosen" because he knows that we are not a perfect union, not then and, I would add, not yet, either. He is humble because he is aware that he has flaws, just like ours.

You could say the same thing about the Jewish people and our leaders as well. The Hebrew Bible is honest about the shortcomings of the first Jews. We know their limits and can fairly call them God's "humble instruments," too. What's more, the Hebrew Bible could have given us a more perfect version of ourselves, this so-called "chosen people," too. Instead, the Hebrew Bible has us study and emulate people of more limited moral strengths, folks like you and me. The Hebrew Bible raises up individuals who do the best they can to navigate the winding paths of life. You can idealize and idolize the past and those who stand at the forefront, but you'd be denying reality if you do so.

So, the question is, "If they are not perfect, then why should I be? Everyone lies, so why can't I?" But as we saw, the Hebrew Bible expects us to do the spiritual heavy lifting of exercising moral judgment. Giving the matter honest thought makes all the difference, and the examined Jewish life begins with Hebrew Bible, as seen through the eyes of the rabbis.

When it comes to the truth of the Hebrew Bible, we have to read it with two sets of eyes—one set on the text and the other on ourselves and the world we occupy. We bring the wisdom of life experience to inform an understanding of the text in making decisions.

# Acknowledgments

This book is about the "Aha!" of Torah study, my reaction when a Jewish teaching makes a difference in how I think or what I do.

I thank the yeshiva rabbis of my Brooklyn childhood; the rabbis, cantors, and teachers of Reform synagogues and youth programs through my teens; and my college, seminary, and school of social work instructors, professors, and classmates. Their teachings provided the foundation of this book.

I also thank my students—children, teens, and adults—especially those who rose early Shabbat mornings to join me in Torah study, as well as the clergy, staff, and members of Congregation Beth Emeth in Albany, New York, and the staff of Family Planning Advocates of New York State, where I direct Concerned Clergy for Choice. I also thank Mary Garofano of Berkshire Medical Center, for her comments on the manuscript and mentorship in medical ethics.

I have special thanks for Jewish Lights Publishing. Stuart M. Matlins, publisher, and Emily Wichland, vice president of Editorial and Production, for their devotion to providing careful attention to all the details as well as the larger decisions. They, along with Amy Wilson, senior vice president of Finance and Operations; Barbara Heise, vice president of Marketing and Sales; and Jenny Buono, book designer and director of Web Marketing and Design, are the heart of Jewish Lights and make possible this book and my previous books, *God in Our Relationships: Spirituality between People from the Teachings of Martin Buber* and *All Politics Is Religious: Speaking Faith to the Media, Policy Makers and Community*. Also at Jewish Lights, I thank Leah Brewer, publicist, and Tim Holtz, director of Design and Production.

Above all, I write with deep affection for my wife, Rabbi Deborah Zecher, and our children, Joshua, Adam, and Miriam, and their abiding and loving support, encouragement, and delight.

# Notes

## Preface

1. Sissela Bok, *Lying: Moral Choice in Public and Private Life,* 2nd ed. (New York: Vintage Books, 1999).
2. *God in Our Relationships: Spirituality between People from the Teachings of Martin Buber* (Woodstock, VT: Jewish Lights Publishing, 2003).
3. *All Politics Is Religious: Speaking Faith to the Media, Policy Makers and Community* (Woodstock, VT: SkyLight Paths Publishing, 2012).

## Chapter 1: The Hebrew Bible Is True

1. Denver Nicks, "Costco Apologizes for Labeling Bibles as Fiction," *Time* (November 20, 2013); http://business.time.com/2013/11/20/costco -apologizes-for-labeling-bibles-as-fiction (accessed January 21, 2016).
2. "The Republican Debate," *New York Times* (November 28, 2007); http:// www.nytimes.com/2007/11/28/us/politics/28debate-transcript.html?page wanted=all (accessed November 30, 2015).

## Chapter 2: The Hebrew Bible and the Truth

1. Cary Funk and Becka A. Alper, "Religion and Science," Pew Research Center (October 22, 2015); http://www.pewinternet.org/2015/10/22/science -and-religion/?utm_source=Pew+Research+Center&utm_campaign=a79d 33fc02-Religion_Weekly_Oct_22_2015&utm_medium=email&utm_term =0_3e953b9b70-a79d33fc02-399920669 (accessed November 30, 2015).
2. In Nahum Sarna, *Exploring Exodus: The Heritage of Biblical Israel* (New York: Schocken, 1986), 68–78.
3. N. Joel Ehrenkranz and Deborah Sampson, "Origin of the Old Testament Plagues: Explications and Implications," *Yale Journal of Biology and Medicine* 81, no. 1 (March 2008): 31–42; http://www.ncbi.nlm .nih.gov/pmc/articles/PMC2442724 (accessed November 30, 2015).
4. Ibid., 31.
5. "On Miracles: A Note on a Poem by Judah ha-Levi," in *Franz Rosenzweig: His Life and Thought,* edited by Nahum N. Glatzer (Indianapolis: Hackett Publishing, 1998), 290.
6. "Campbell's Accused by F.T.C. of Putting Marbles in TV Soup," *New York Times* (March 25, 1969); http://query.nytimes.com/mem/archive /pdf?res=980DE2DC153AEE34BC4D51DFB5668382679EDE (accessed, November 30, 2015).
7. Nehama Leibowitz, *New Studies in the Weekly Parashat: Shemot,* vol. 1 (New York: Lambda Publishers, 2010), 334.
8. Rashi to Leviticus 19:36.

## Chapter 3: The White Lie

1. Rashi to Genesis 18:12.
2. Samson Raphael Hirsch, in W. Gunther Plaut and David E. S. Stern, eds., *The Torah: A Modern Commentary*, revised edition (New York: URJ Press, 2005), 143.
3. Rachel Martin, "Learning the Hard Truth about Lying," National Public Radio; http://www.npr.org/2015/03/08/391610430/learning-the-hard-truth-about-lying (accessed November 30, 2015).

## Chapter 4: Embellishment

1. Dan Ariely, *The (Honest) Truth about Dishonesty: How We Lie to Everyone—Especially Ourselves* (New York: Harper, 2013).
2. Rashi to Genesis 3:3.
3. Rashi to Genesis 3:6
4. Rashi to Genesis 3:2.
5. Rashi to Genesis 4:1.
6. Stephen Colbert, interview by Nathan Rabin, *A.V. Club*, January 25, 2006; http://www.avclub.com/article/stephen-colbert-13970 (accessed November 30, 2015).
7. Charles Seife, *Proofiness: The Dark Side of Mathematical Deception* (New York: Viking, 2010), in "Lies, Damned Lies, and 'Proofiness,'" National Public Radio, September 20, 2010; http://www.npr.org/templates/story/story.php?storyId=129972868 (accessed January 19, 2015).
8. Ibid.

## Chapter 5: The Half-Truth

1. Abravanel to Exodus 3:18.
2. Hizkuni to Exodus 3:18.
3. Nehama Leibowitz, *New Studies in the Weekly Parasha: Shemot*, vol. 1 (New York: Lambda Publishers, 2010), 94–95.
4. Rashi to Genesis 31:19.

## Chapter 6: The Benevolent/Paternalistic Lie

1. Rashi to Genesis 22:5.
2. Rashi to Genesis 22:6.
3. Rashi to Genesis 23:2.
4. Rashi to Genesis 22:12.
5. Bok, *Lying*, 210.

## Chapter 7: Little Lies, Big Headaches

1. Bok, *Lying*, 31.

## Chapter 8: Lying to Protect Oneself, Part 1

1. Bruce Feiler, "The Stories That Bind Us," *New York Times* (March 15, 2013); http://www.nytimes.com/2013/03/17/fashion/the-family-stories-that-bind-us-this-life.html?_r=0 (accessed November 30, 2015).

2. Rashi to Genesis 12:13.
3. Nahmanides to Genesis 12:10.
4. Radak to Genesis 12:17.

## Chapter 9: Lying to Protect Oneself, Part 2

1. Facebook page of Burlington Liars Club; https://www.facebook.com /burlingtonliarsclub/ (accessed November 30, 2015).
2. Bok, *Lying*, 121.
3. Rashi to Genesis 50:16.
4. Sforno to Genesis 50:16.
5. Rashi to Genesis 50:21.
6. Carl Zimmer, "Devious Butterflies, Full-Throated Frogs and Other Liars," *New York Times* (December 26, 2006); http://www.nytimes .com/2006/12/26/science/26lying.html (accessed November 30, 2015).
7. Megan Garber, "How to Catch a Liar on the Internet," *Atlantic* (September 2013); http://www.theatlantic.com/magazine/archive/2013/09/the-way-we -lie-now/309431/ (accessed January 21, 2016).
8. Pamela Meyer, "Can You Learn to Spot a Liar?" National Public Radio (June 20, 2014); http://www.npr.org/templates/transcript/transcript.php ?storyId=321797472 (accessed November 30, 2015).

## Chapter 10: Lying to Get Ahead

1. Rashi to Genesis 25:22.
2. Rashi to Genesis 27:24.
3. See also W. Gunther Plaut, "The Strange Blessing: A Modern Midrash on Genesis 27," *CCAR Journal* (June 1960): 30ff.
4. Dan Barry, "The High Brought Low: Cheating Hearts and Lying Resumes," *New York Times* (December 18, 1997); http://www.nytimes .com/1997/12/14/weekinreview/the-high-brought-low-cheating-hearts-and -lying-resumes.html (accessed January 16, 2016).

## Chapter 11: Lying to Hurt Others

1. Rashi to Genesis 39:11.
2. Ibn Ezra to Genesis 39:19.

## Chapter 12: The Noble Truth and the Noble Lie

1. Rashi to Genesis 18:17.
2. J. H. Hertz, *Pentateuch and Haftoras: Hebrew Text, English Translation and Commentary* (London: Soncino Press, 1993), 208.
3. Ibid.
4. Nehamah Leibowitz, *New Studies in the Weekly Parasha: Shemot*, vol. 2 (New York: Lambda Publishers, 2010), 34–35.
5. Nahum Sarna, *Exploring Exodus: The Heritage of Biblical Israel* (New York: Schocken, 1986), 25–26.
6. Ibid., 25.

## Chapter 13: Instruments of Decision

1. "Our Latest Fact-Checks," PolitiFact; http://www.politifact.com/truth
-o-meter/statements/ (accessed November 30, 2015).

## Chapter 14: Medical Ethics: Personal Decisions and Jewish Perspectives

1. Jewish Medical Ethics; http://www.daneisenberg.com/ (accessed November 30, 2015).
2. Erich Fromm, *You Shall Be as Gods: A Radical Interpretation of the Old Testament and Its Tradition* (Austin, TX: Holt, Rinehart and Winston, 1996), 71.
3. Rashi to Genesis 3:7.
4. Rashi to Genesis 4:3.
5. "Reform Judaism: A Centenary Perspective," Central Conference of American Rabbis; http://ccarnet.org/rabbis-speak/platforms/reform-judaism -centenary-perspective/ (accessed November 30, 2015).

## Chapter 15: A Rulebook for Living or a Framework for Deciding?

1. Michael and Sharon Strassfeld and Richard Siegel, *The First Jewish Catalog* (Philadelphia: Jewish Publication Society, 1965).
2. Eugene Borowitz, *Choices in Modern Jewish Thought: A Partisan Guide* (New York: Behrman House, 1983), 271.

## Epilogue: The Examined Jewish Life

1. Emily Upton, "George Washington Never Chopped Down a Cherry Tree," *Today I Found Out* (September 4, 2013); http://www.today ifoundout.com/index.php/2013/09/george-washington-never-chopped -down-a-cherry-tree/ https://georgewashingtoninn.wordpress.com/2009 /03/21/the-legend-of-the-cherry-tree/ (accessed November 30, 2015).
2. Abraham Lincoln, "Address to the New Jersey State Senate," Trenton, New Jersey, February 21, 1861; http://www.abrahamlincolnonline.org /lincoln/speeches/trenton1.htm (accessed November 30, 2015).

# For Further Reading

## Torah Study

### Introductory

Fields, Rabbi Harvey J. *A Torah Commentary for Our Times*. New York: UAHC Press, 1990.

Plaut, Rabbi W. Gunther, and David E. S. Stein, eds. *The Torah: A Modern Commentary*. 2nd ed. New York: URJ Press, 2005.

### Intermediate

Bialik, Hayyim Nahman, and Yehoshua Hana Ravnitzky, eds., and William G. Braude, trans. *The Book of Legends/Sefer Ha-Aggadah: Legends from the Talmud and Midrash*. New York: Schocken, 1992.

Carasik, Michael. *The Commentator's Bible: The JPS Miqra'ot Gedolot*. Philadelphia: Jewish Publication Society, 2005.

Leibowitz, Nehamah. *New Studies in the Weekly Parasha*. New York: Lambda Publishers, 2010.

## Truth, Falsehood, Free Will

Ariely, Dan Ariely. *The Honest Truth about Dishonesty: How We Lie to Everyone—Especially Ourselves*. New York: Harper Perennial, 2013.

Bok, Sissela. *Lying: Moral Choice in Public and Private Life*. 2nd ed. New York: Vintage, 1999.

Dratch, Mark. "Nothing But the Truth." *Judaism* (Spring 1988): 218–228.

Friedman, Hershey H., and Abraham C. Weisel, Esq. "Should Moral Individuals Ever Lie? Insights from Jewish Law." Jewish Law. http://www.jlaw.com/Articles/hf_LyingPermissible.html (accessed December 6, 2015).

"Types of Speech." My Jewish Learning. http://www.myjewishlearning.com/article/types-of-speech/# (accessed December 6, 2015).

Winston, David. "Free Will." In Arthur A. Cohen and Paul Mendes-Flohr, eds., *Twentieth-Century Jewish Religious Thought*, 269–274. Philadelphia: Jewish Publication Society, 2009.

Zivotofsky, Ari. "Perspectives on Truthfulness in the Jewish Tradition." *Judaism* (Summer 1993): 267–288.

## Jewish Perspectives on Medical Ethics

Eisenberg, Dr. Daniel. http://www.daneisenberg.com/ (accessed December 6, 2015). The website lists a variety of excellent articles about Judaism and medical ethics.

"Jewish Bioethics." My Jewish Learning. http://www.myjewishlearning.com/article/jewish-bioethics/ (accessed December 6, 2015).

## *Bible Study / Midrash*

**Passing Life's Tests:** Spiritual Reflections on the Trial of Abraham, the Binding of Isaac  *By Rabbi Bradley Shavit Artson, DHL*
Invites us to use this powerful tale as a tool for our own soul wrestling, to confront our existential sacrifices and enable us to face—and surmount—life's tests.
6 x 9, 176 pp, Quality PB, 978-1-58023-631-7  **$18.99**

**Speaking Torah:** Spiritual Teachings from around the Maggid's Table—in Two Volumes  *By Arthur Green, with Ebn Leader, Ariel Evan Mayse and Or N. Rose*
The most powerful Hasidic teachings made accessible—from some of the world's preeminent authorities on Jewish thought and spirituality.
Volume 1—6 x 9, 512 pp, HC, 978-1-58023-668-3  **$34.99**
Volume 2—6 x 9, 448 pp, HC, 978-1-58023-694-2  **$34.99**

**A Partner in Holiness:** Deepening Mindfulness, Practicing Compassion and Enriching Our Lives through the Wisdom of R. Levi Yitzhak of Berdichev's *Kedushat Levi*
*By Rabbi Jonathan P. Slater, DMin; Foreword by Arthur Green; Preface by Rabby Nancy Flam*
Contemporary mindfulness and classical Hasidic spirituality are brought together to inspire a satisfying spiritual life of practice.
Volume 1—6 x 9, 336 pp, HC, 978-1-58023-794-9  **$35.00**
Volume 2—6 x 9, 288 pp, HC, 978-1-58023-795-6  **$35.00**

**The Genesis of Leadership:** What the Bible Teaches Us about Vision, Values and Leading Change  *By Rabbi Nathan Laufer; Foreword by Senator Joseph I. Lieberman*
6 x 9, 288 pp, Quality PB, 978-1-58023-352-1  **$18.99**

**Hineini in Our Lives:** Learning How to Respond to Others through 14 Biblical Texts and Personal Stories  *By Dr. Norman J. Cohen*  6 x 9, 240 pp, Quality PB, 978-1-58023-274-6  **$18.99**

**Masking and Unmasking Ourselves:** Interpreting Biblical Texts on Clothing & Identity  *By Dr. Norman J. Cohen*  6 x 9, 224 pp, HC, 978-1-58023-461-0  **$24.99**
Quality PB, 978-1-58023-839-7  **$18.99**

**The Messiah and the Jews:** Three Thousand Years of Tradition, Belief and Hope
*By Rabbi Elaine Rose Glickman; Foreword by Rabbi Neil Gillman, PhD*
*Preface by Rabbi Judith Z. Abrams, PhD*  6 x 9, 192 pp, Quality PB, 978-1-58023-690-4  **$16.99**

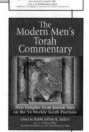

**The Modern Men's Torah Commentary:** New Insights from Jewish Men on the 54 Weekly Torah Portions  *Edited by Rabbi Jeffrey K. Salkin*
6 x 9, 368 pp, HC, 978-1-58023-395-8  **$24.99**

**Moses and the Journey to Leadership:** Timeless Lessons of Effective Management from the Bible and Today's Leaders  *By Dr. Norman J. Cohen*
6 x 9, 240 pp, Quality PB, 978-1-58023-351-4  **$18.99**; HC, 978-1-58023-227-2  **$21.99**

**The Other Talmud—The *Yerushalmi*:** Unlocking the Secrets of *The Talmud of Israel* for Judaism Today  *By Rabbi Judith Z. Abrams, PhD*
6 x 9, 256 pp, HC, 978-1-58023-463-4  **$24.99**

**Sage Tales:** Wisdom and Wonder from the Rabbis of the Talmud
*By Rabbi Burton L. Visotzky*
6 x 9, 256 pp, Quality PB, 978-1-58023-791-8  **$19.99**; HC, 978-1-58023-456-6  **$24.99**

**The Torah Revolution:** Fourteen Truths That Changed the World
*By Rabbi Reuven Hammer, PhD*  6 x 9, 240 pp, Quality PB, 978-1-58023-789-5  **$18.99**
HC, 978-1-58023-457-3  **$24.99**

**The Wisdom of Judaism:** An Introduction to the Values of the Talmud
*By Rabbi Dov Peretz Elkins*  6 x 9, 192 pp, Quality PB, 978-1-58023-327-9  **$16.99**

# Inspiration

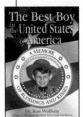

## The Best Boy in the United States of America
A Memoir of Blessings and Kisses  *By Dr. Ron Wolfson*
Will resonate with anyone seeking to shape stronger families and communities and live a life of joy and purpose.  6 x 9, 192 pp, HC, 978-1-58023-838-0  **$19.99**

## The Chutzpah Imperative: Empowering Today's Jews for a Life That Matters  *By Rabbi Edward Feinstein; Foreword by Rabbi Laura Geller*
A new view of chutzpah as Jewish self-empowerment to be God's partner and repair the world. Reveals Judaism's ancient message, its deepest purpose and most precious treasures.  6 x 9, 192 pp, HC, 978-1-58023-792-5  **$21.99**

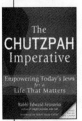

## Judaism's Ten Best Ideas: A Brief Guide for Seekers
*By Rabbi Arthur Green, PhD*  A highly accessible introduction to Judaism's greatest contributions to civilization, drawing on Jewish mystical tradition and the author's experience.  4½ x 6½, 112 pp, Quality PB, 978-1-58023-803-8  **$9.99**

## The Empty Chair: Finding Hope and Joy—Timeless Wisdom from a Hasidic Master, Rebbe Nachman of Breslov  *Adapted by Moshe Mykoff and the Breslov Research Institute*
4 x 6, 128 pp, Deluxe PB w/ flaps, 978-1-879045-67-5  **$9.99**

## The Gentle Weapon: Prayers for Everyday and Not-So-Everyday Moments—
Timeless Wisdom from the Teachings of the Hasidic Master Rebbe Nachman of Breslov  *Adapted by Moshe Mykoff and S. C. Mizrahi, together with the Breslov Research Institute*
4 x 6, 144 pp, Deluxe PB w/ flaps, 978-1-58023-022-3  **$9.99**

## God Whispers: Stories of the Soul, Lessons of the Heart  *By Rabbi Karyn D. Kedar*
6 x 9, 176 pp, Quality PB, 978-1-58023-088-9  **$16.99**

## God's To-Do List: 103 Ways to Be an Angel and Do God's Work on Earth
*By Dr. Ron Wolfson*  6 x 9, 144 pp, Quality PB, 978-1-58023-301-9  **$16.99**

## Happiness and the Human Spirit: The Spirituality of Becoming the Best You Can Be
*By Rabbi Abraham J. Twerski, MD*
6 x 9, 176 pp, Quality PB, 978-1-58023-404-7  **$16.99**; HC, 978-1-58023-343-9  **$19.99**

## Life's Daily Blessings: Inspiring Reflections on Gratitude and Joy for Every Day,
Based on Jewish Wisdom  *By Rabbi Kerry M. Olitzky*
4½ x 6½, 368 pp, Quality PB, 978-1-58023-396-5  **$16.99**

## Sacred Intentions: Morning Inspiration to Strengthen the Spirit, Based on Jewish Wisdom
*By Rabbi Kerry M. Olitzky and Rabbi Lori Forman-Jacobi*
4½ x 6½, 448 pp, Quality PB, 978-1-58023-061-2  **$16.99**

## The Seven Questions You're Asked in Heaven: Reviewing and Renewing Your
Life on Earth  *By Dr. Ron Wolfson*  6 x 9, 176 pp, Quality PB, 978-1-58023-407-8  **$16.99**

# Kabbalah / Mysticism

## Walking the Path of the Jewish Mystic: How to Expand Your
Awareness and Transform Your Life  *By Rabbi Yoel Glick*
A unique guide to the nature of both physical and spiritual reality.
6 x 9, 224 pp, Quality PB, 978-1-58023-843-4  **$18.99**

## Ehyeh: A Kabbalah for Tomorrow
*By Rabbi Arthur Green, PhD*  6 x 9, 224 pp, Quality PB, 978-1-58023-213-5  **$18.99**

## The Gift of Kabbalah: Discovering the Secrets of Heaven, Renewing Your Life on Earth
*By Tamar Frankiel, PhD*  6 x 9, 256 pp, Quality PB, 978-1-58023-141-1  **$18.99**

## Jewish Mysticism and the Spiritual Life: Classical Texts, Contemporary
Reflections  *Edited by Dr. Lawrence Fine, Dr. Eitan Fishbane and Rabbi Or N. Rose*
6 x 9, 256 pp, Quality PB, 978-1-58023-719-2  **$18.99**

## Seek My Face: A Jewish Mystical Theology  *By Rabbi Arthur Green, PhD*
6 x 9, 304 pp, Quality PB, 978-1-58023-130-5  **$19.95**

## Zohar: Annotated & Explained  *Translation & Annotation by Dr. Daniel C. Matt*
*Foreword by Andrew Harvey*  5½ x 8½, 176 pp, Quality PB, 978-1-893361-51-5  **$18.99**
*(A book from SkyLight Paths, Jewish Lights' sister imprint)*

See also *The Way Into Jewish Mystical Tradition* in The Way Into... Series

# *Spirituality*

## The Rhythms of Jewish Living
### A Sephardic Exploration of Judaism's Spirituality
*By Rabbi Marc D. Angel, PhD* Reclaims the natural, balanced and insightful teachings of Sephardic Judaism that can and should imbue modern Jewish spirituality.
6 x 9, 208 pp, Quality PB, 978-1-58023-834-2 **$18.99**

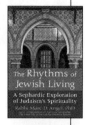

## God and the Big Bang, 2nd Edition
### Discovering Harmony between Science and Spirituality
*By Daniel C. Matt* Updated and expanded. Draws on the insights of physics and Kabbalah to uncover the sense of wonder and oneness that connects humankind with the universe and God. 6 x 9, 224 pp, Quality PB, 978-1-58023-836-6 **$18.99**

## Amazing Chesed: Living a Grace-Filled Judaism
*By Rabbi Rami Shapiro* Drawing from ancient and contemporary, traditional and non-traditional Jewish wisdom, reclaims the idea of grace in Judaism.
6 x 9, 176 pp, Quality PB, 978-1-58023-624-9 **$16.99**

## Perennial Wisdom for the Spiritually Independent: Sacred Teachings—
Annotated & Explained *Annotation by Rabbi Rami Shapiro; Foreword by Richard Rohr* Weaves sacred texts and teachings from the world's major religions into a coherent exploration of the five core questions at the heart of every religion's search.
5½ x 8½, 336 pp, Quality PB, 978-1-59473-515-8 **$16.99**\*

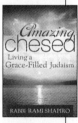

**A Book of Life:** Embracing Judaism as a Spiritual Practice
*By Rabbi Michael Strassfeld* 6 x 9, 544 pp, Quality PB, 978-1-58023-247-0 **$24.99**

**Bringing the Psalms to Life:** How to Understand and Use the Book of Psalms
*By Rabbi Daniel F. Polish, PhD* 6 x 9, 208 pp, Quality PB, 978-1-58023-157-2 **$18.99**

**Does the Soul Survive? 2nd Edition:** A Jewish Journey to Belief in Afterlife, Past Lives & Living with Purpose *By Rabbi Elie Kaplan Spitz; Foreword by Brian L. Weiss, MD*
6 x 9, 288 pp, Quality PB, 978-1-58023-818-2 **$18.99**

**First Steps to a New Jewish Spirit:** Reb Zalman's Guide to Recapturing the Intimacy & Ecstasy in Your Relationship with God *By Rabbi Zalman Schachter-Shalomi (z"l) with Donald Gropman*
6 x 9, 144 pp, Quality PB, 978-1-58023-182-4 **$16.95**

**Foundations of Sephardic Spirituality:** The Inner Life of Jews of the Ottoman Empire
*By Rabbi Marc D. Angel, PhD* 6 x 9, 224 pp, Quality PB, 978-1-58023-341-5 **$18.99**

**The God Upgrade:** Finding Your 21st-Century Spirituality in Judaism's 5,000-Year-Old Tradition *By Rabbi Jamie Korngold; Foreword by Rabbi Harold M. Schulweis*
6 x 9, 176 pp, Quality PB, 978-1-58023-443-6 **$15.99**

**The Jewish Lights Spirituality Handbook:** A Guide to Understanding, Exploring & Living a Spiritual Life *Edited by Stuart M. Matlins*
6 x 9, 456 pp, Quality PB, 978-1-58023-093-3 **$19.99**

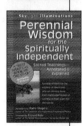

**Jewish with Feeling:** A Guide to Meaningful Jewish Practice
*By Rabbi Zalman Schachter-Shalomi (z"l) with Joel Segel*
5½ x 8½, 288 pp, Quality PB, 978-1-58023-691-1 **$19.99**

**Judaism, Physics and God:** Searching for Sacred Metaphors in a Post-Einstein World
*By Rabbi David W. Nelson*
6 x 9, 352 pp, Quality PB, inc. reader's discussion guide, 978-1-58023-306-4 **$18.99**
HC, 352 pp, 978-1-58023-252-4 **$24.99**

**Repentance:** The Meaning and Practice of Teshuvah
*By Dr. Louis E. Newman; Foreword by Rabbi Harold M. Schulweis; Preface by Rabbi Karyn D. Kedar*
6 x 9, 256 pp, Quality PB, 978-1-58023-718-5 **$18.99**

**Tanya, the Masterpiece of Hasidic Wisdom:** Selections Annotated & Explained
*Translation & Annotation by Rabbi Rami Shapiro; Foreword by Rabbi Zalman Schachter-Shalomi (z"l)*
5½ x 8½, 240 pp, Quality PB, 978-1-59473-275-1 **$18.99**\*

**These Are the Words, 2nd Edition:** A Vocabulary of Jewish Spiritual Life
*By Rabbi Arthur Green, PhD* 6 x 9, 320 pp, Quality PB, 978-1-58023-494-8 **$19.99**

**Your Word Is Fire:** The Hasidic Masters on Contemplative Prayer
*Edited and translated by Rabbi Arthur Green, PhD, and Barry W. Holtz*
6 x 9, 160 pp, Quality PB, 978-1-879045-25-5 **$16.99**

\**A book from SkyLight Paths, Jewish Lights' sister imprint*

## About Jewish Lights

People of all faiths and backgrounds yearn for books that attract, engage, educate, and spiritually inspire.

Our principal goal is to stimulate thought and help all people learn about who the Jewish People are, where they come from, and what the future can be made to hold. While people of our diverse Jewish heritage are the primary audience, our books speak to people in the Christian world as well and will broaden their understanding of Judaism and the roots of their own faith.

We bring to you authors who are at the forefront of spiritual thought and experience. While each has something different to say, they all say it in a voice that you can hear.

Our books are designed to welcome you and then to engage, stimulate, and inspire. We judge our success not only by whether or not our books are beautiful and commercially successful, but by whether or not they make a difference in your life.

For your information and convenience, at the back of this book we have provided a list of other Jewish Lights books you might find interesting and useful. They cover all the categories of your life:

| | |
|---|---|
| Bar/Bat Mitzvah | Life Cycle |
| Bible Study / Midrash | Meditation |
| Children's Books | Men's Interest |
| Congregation Resources | Parenting |
| Current Events / History | Prayer / Ritual / Sacred Practice |
| Ecology / Environment | Social Justice |
| Fiction: Mystery, Science Fiction | Spirituality |
| Grief / Healing | Theology / Philosophy |
| Holidays / Holy Days | Travel |
| Inspiration | Twelve Steps |
| Kabbalah / Mysticism / Enneagram | Women's Interest |

Stuart M. Matlins, Publisher

*Or phone, fax, mail or email to:* **JEWISH LIGHTS Publishing**
Sunset Farm Offices, Route 4 • P.O. Box 237 • Woodstock, Vermont 05091
Tel: (802) 457-4000 • Fax: (802) 457-4004 • www.jewishlights.com
**Credit card orders:** **(800) 962-4544** (8:30AM–5:30PM EST Monday–Friday)
Generous discounts on quantity orders. SATISFACTION GUARANTEED. Prices subject to change.

**For more information about each book, visit our website at www.jewishlights.com.**